LEARN CHINESE
VOCABULARY
FOR BEGINNERS

NEW HSK LEVEL 1 VOCABULARLY BOOK
MASTER 500 WORDS IN CONTEXT

Chinese • Pinyin • English

LingLing

www.linglingmandarin.com

ACKNOWLEDGEMENTS

My gratitude goes to my wonderful students who study
Mandarin with me – you have inspired my writing and
had given me valuable feedback to complete this book.
Your support is deeply appreciated!

Special thanks go to my husband Phil, who motivated my
creation and assisted with the editing and proofreading
of the book.

Access FREE Audio!

FOR FULL INSTRUCTIONS
SEE <u>ACCESS AUDIO CHAPTER (P.103)</u>

TABLE OF CONTENTS

千　里　之　行
qiān　lǐ　zhī　xíng

始　于　足　下
shǐ　yú　zú　xià

A journey of a thousand miles
begins with a single step

- LAOZI -

INTRODUCTION

Thank you, dear reader, for purchasing this book. If you've just started learning Chinese, I wish you a warm welcome to the beginning of your learning journey and hope it is an enjoyable, enriching, and fulfilling one! There will be challenges along the way; my aim is to help you overcome those by providing you with helpful tips and resources that will make learning fun and give you great insights into both the Chinese language and culture.

WHAT IS THIS BOOK?

This book focuses on building a solid foundation for Chinese language communication. The keywords covered in the vocabulary section of this book make up the New HSK Level 1. More on that later, don't worry if you don't know what that is or have no intention of studying specifically for it. The keywords, plus additional words used in the examples provided, form the basis of the most common and fundamental vocabulary required for communicating in Chinese.

The keywords are provided in alphabetical order according to the pinyin and include:

- Simplified Chinese characters - as used in Mainland China
- Pinyin - pronunciation aid
- English definition
- Complete sentence example showing usage
- Full English translation and downloadable audio

Where multiple definitions exist for a single word, full-sentence examples are provided for each definition.

As a special bonus, I have also included an entire section dedicated to mastering numbers in Chinese. I have used this with many of my beginner students, who are often surprised by how quickly they can count up to big numbers in Chinese when they learn the rules of counting in Chinese.

HOW WILL IT HELP?

Learning a word in isolation will only take you so far; you need to know how to use it correctly. The examples in this book will help you master the vocabulary and appropriate usage and introduce you to common sentence patterns and related language to kick-start your journey toward mastering Chinese. You will build a strong foundation of everyday Chinese words. So whether you intend to take the HSK exam or not, you will be well on your way to being conversational in Chinese.

FREE DOWNLOADABLE AUDIO

Great news! The audio files for this book can be downloaded absolutely FREE, my gift to you, beloved readers who purchase this book. You can access the audio file via the link provided on the "Access Audio File" page toward the back of this book (see Table of Contents). The audio includes all the Chinese keywords and definitions, full sentence examples, and English translations covered in the book. It also includes examples of numbers from the "Master Chinese Numbers" chapter.

MASTER CHINESE NUMBERS

The great news just keeps coming! In addition to all the vocabulary, sentence examples, and free audio that you get with this book, I have also included a special bonus chapter that will teach you step-by-step how to say any number from zero to a billion (in fact with the rules and vocabulary provided, even a trillion).

LEARNING VIDEOS AND CONTENT

You can also find many learning videos that cover much of the vocabulary in this book and more on my YouTube channel (LingLing Mandarin). I also post Chinese learning content on Instagram (@LingLingMandarin) and Pinterest (@LingMandarin), so if you're looking for regular content to keep you motivated and enhance your Chinese learning, then I encourage you to find me on your platform of choice.

Why learn chinese?

Chinese is one of the most varied, dynamic, and artistic languages and has developed over 3500 years. It is one of the most spoken languages in the world. Learning Chinese will open the door to new opportunities in life, travel, business, and personal development.

About the chinese language

Many people consider Chinese to be one of the hardest languages to learn for native English speakers. While it will take a good amount of effort and time, it is an enriching and rewarding experience. Many students even find it not as challenging as they first thought. Consider Chinese grammar; it is relatively simple compared to many Indo-European languages. Verbs have no tense, and nouns have no gender or plurality variations.

The key to learning Chinese, especially spoken Chinese, is through the study of words in context (no need for hours of complex grammar classes). You will also most effectively learn key sentence patterns this way as well as vocabulary.

New hsk level 1

HSK is short for Hanyu Shuiping Kaoshi (Mandarin Level Examination) - an international standard skill test for non-native Chinese speakers officially introduced by the Chinese government and organized by the Chinese Education Ministry Hanban/Confucius Institutes. The old HSK Standard has 6 levels; however, starting July 2021, the New HSK standard (HSK 3.0) will replace it. The new version has 9 levels, with a more specific classification system, including both levels and bands. Compared to its predecessor, it is upgraded and expanded. The number of words required for each level also increased.

As a general learner, you only need to focus from level 1 to level 6 to become an effective Mandarin speaker. Level 7 and above is designed specifically for advanced learners, for example, those who intend to progress into a Masters or PhD program in Chinese language study.

HOW TO USE THIS BOOK

Here are some tips to use this book most effectively:

- **Stick to a fixed routine.** For example, master ten vocabularies per day or week - you pick a number and schedule that suits you but most importantly, stick to it.

- **Read aloud**, especially the sentence examples. Imagine the context in your head when reading.

- **Test** yourself by covering the Pinyin and English. If you can read and understand the Chinese on its own, you have memorized it.

- **Listen** to the audio. Make sure you capture the pronunciation of each word, and then practice and keep listening until you can comprehend the audio without the help of the book.

- **Review** as often as you can. Repetition is the mother of skill!

- **Create** your own sentence examples. Practice speaking them aloud, and if possible, use them with a language partner. One becomes a true master through creation!

BELIEVE IN YOURSELF

Believe in yourself and have confidence! Never be afraid of making mistakes. In real life, even advanced learners and native speakers make mistakes! Plus, mistakes only make us grow quicker! Never let mistakes put you off. Instead, be bold, embrace and learn from mistakes! Remember, success and achievement come from confidence, perseverance, and a never-give-up attitude! Just like the famous Chinese idiom:

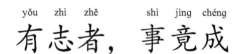

Nothing is Impossible to a Willing Heart

TONES AND PINYIN

CHINESE AS A TONAL LANGUAGE

You have probably heard that Mandarin Chinese is a "tonal language," but what does this mean? Many characters have the same basic sound in Mandarin Chinese; therefore, we use tones when speaking to differentiate words. In Mandarin Chinese, there are four tones plus a neutral "tone":

First Tone	High (and flat)	▬	Pitch starts higher and stays high (no change in tone) - sound is slightly more drawn out
Second Tone	Rising	╱	Pitch starts low and ends slightly high
Third Tone	Falling then Rising	╲╱	Pitch starts neutral, dips to lower, then rises to a higher pitch
Fourth Tone	Falling	╲	Pitch starts slightly higher then falls quickly to a lower tone
Neutral Tone	Neutral		Neutral pronunciation with no change to pitch

Let's take a look at an example of how the tone determines the word being spoken; the following words all use the base syllable "ma" but with different tones applied (listen to the audio for pronunciation):

Character	妈	麻	马	骂	吗
Pinyin	mā	má	mǎ	mà	ma
Meaning	mother	hemp	horse	scold	question particle
Tone	first	second	third	fourth	neutral

PINYIN

Pinyin, literally "spelled sounds," is the official romanization system for Mandarin Chinese in Mainland China. It is the most commonly used phonetic system for writing Mandarin using the Latin alphabet. Since Chinese is not a phonetic language and has no alphabet, Pinyin can help accelerate Chinese learning.

Pinyin is typically displayed above, or sometimes below, the actual Chinese characters.

pīn yīn
拼音　　拼音
　　　　pīn yīn

It provides two important pieces of information to the reader; firstly, the basic sound/syllable of the character, and secondly, the tone. The basic sound can be broken down into an "initial" and a "final." The tone is denoted through one of four possible accent marks above the Latin characters. For example, the word for China (composed of two characters):

Character	Initial		Final		Tone		Syllable
中	zh	+	ong	+	ˉ	=	zhōng
国	g	+	uo	+	ˊ	=	guó

It is important to know and remember that Pinyin is not English (or any other language using the Latin alphabet)! Some resources provide approximations of Pinyin sounds to English, but these do not always accurately capture the nuances and differences in pronunciation. Use the audio provided for this book and listen to other native speakers to truly hone and master pronunciation.

Pinyin is also frequently used as an input method on phones and computers for Chinese. A user may type in Pinyin and select the correct Chinese characters from a list of matching ones.

ni'hao|

| 1 你好　　2 你号　　3 拟好　　4 倪浩

1

MASTER CHINESE NUMBERS

ZERO TO A BILLION

ZERO TO TEN

The numbers from one to ten form the basis of all the other numbers in Chinese. So if you can count to ten, then following the rules laid out in this chapter, you'll have no problems saying much bigger numbers!

Here are the numbers from zero to ten in Chinese:

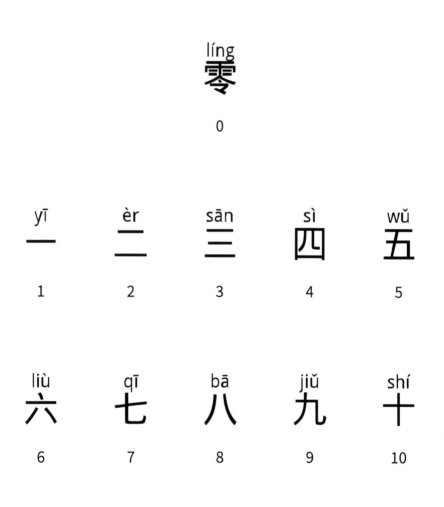

líng
零
0

yī — 1

èr 二 2

sān 三 3

sì 四 4

wǔ 五 5

liù 六 6

qī 七 7

bā 八 8

jiǔ 九 9

shí 十 10

THE NON-10S RULE

Counting in Chinese follows basic mathematical principles. Just like adding 10 and 1 equals 11; so 11 in Chinese is 十一 (十 plus 一). Imagine saying "ten-one" in English - no need to learn special numbers for 11 to 19.

See the table provided for how this rule works when counting from 11 to 19. The rule continues to apply for 21 to 29, 31 to 39, 41 to 49, and so on.

shí yī 十一 11	=	shí 十 10	+	yī 一 1	
shí èr 十二 12	=	shí 十 10	+	èr 二 2	
shí sān 十三 13	=	shí 十 10	+	sān 三 3	
shí sì 十四 14	=	shí 十 10	+	sì 四 4	
shí wǔ 十五 15	=	shí 十 10	+	wǔ 五 5	
shí liù 十六 16	=	shí 十 10	+	liù 六 6	
shí qī 十七 17	=	shí 十 10	+	qī 七 7	
shí bā 十八 18	=	shí 十 10	+	bā 八 8	
shí jiǔ 十九 19	=	shí 十 10	+	jiǔ 九 9	

THE RULE OF 10s

Just like the number 20 is a multiplication of 2 and 10, so 20 in Chinese is 二十 (二 multiplied by 十), imagine saying it as "two-tens" in English.

二十 (èr shí) 20	=	二 (èr) 2 x 十 (shí) 10
三十 (sān shí) 30	=	三 (sān) 3 x 十 (shí) 10
四十 (sì shí) 40	=	四 (sì) 4 x 十 (shí) 10
五十 (wǔ shí) 50	=	五 (wǔ) 5 x 十 (shí) 10
六十 (liù shí) 60	=	六 (liù) 6 x 十 (shí) 10
七十 (qī shí) 70	=	七 (qī) 7 x 十 (shí) 10
八十 (bā shí) 80	=	八 (bā) 8 x 十 (shí) 10
九十 (jiǔ shí) 90	=	九 (jiǔ) 9 x 十 (shí) 10

EXAMPLES: UP TO 99

Using the rules and information provided so far, you should be able say any number up to 99 and you only need to know 10 words to do so (11 if you include zero - don't forget zero, you will be needing it later).

Let's take a look at a couple of examples that we can already say:

EXAMPLE A1: 26

èr shí liù
二 十 六   =   èr * shí   +   liù
26   二 20 十   六 6

EXAMPLE A2: 34

sān shí sì
三 十 四   =   sān * shí   +   sì
34   三 30 十   四 4

EXAMPLE A3: 57

wǔ shí qī
五 十 七   =   wǔ * shí   +   qī
57   五 50 十   七 7

EXAMPLE A4: 85

bā shí wǔ
八 十 五   =   bā * shí   +   wǔ
85   八 80 十   五 5

EXAMPLE A5: 99

jiǔ shí jiǔ
九 十 九   =   jiǔ * shí   +   jiǔ
99   九 90 十   九 9

BIGGER NUMBERS

As the same rules apply to all other numbers in Chinese, you just need to **master the unit names** from ten onward, then you will be able to count much bigger numbers with ease!

shí 十	Ten	X0
bǎi 百	Hundred	X00
qiān 千	Thousand	X,000
wàn 万	Ten Thousand	X0,000
shí　wàn 十　万	Hundred Thousand	X00,000
bǎi　wàn 百　万	Million	X,000,000
qiān　wàn 千　万	Ten Million	X0,000,000
yì 亿	Hundred Million	X00,000,000
shí　yì 十　亿	Billion	X,000,000,000

EXAMPLE B1: 160

shí yì 十亿 Billion	yì 亿 Hundred Million	qiān wàn 千万 Ten Million	bǎi wàn 百万 Million	shí wàn 十万 Hundred Thousand	wàn 万 Ten Thousand	qiān 千 Thousand	bǎi 百 Hundred	shí 十 Ten	
							1 yī bǎi 一百	6 liù shí 六十	0

By knowing each unit name, plus using the rules provided, for 160 we get:

160 = 一百六十 (yī bǎi liù shí)

100 (一百 yī bǎi) + 60 (六十 liù shí)

EXAMPLE B2: 1,273

shí yì 十亿 Billion	yì 亿 Hundred Million	qiān wàn 千万 Ten Million	bǎi wàn 百万 Million	shí wàn 十万 Hundred Thousand	wàn 万 Ten Thousand	qiān 千 Thousand	bǎi 百 Hundred	shí 十 Ten	
						1 yī qiān 一千	2 èr bǎi 二百	7 qī shí 七十	3 sān 三

1,273 = 一千二百七十三 (yī qiān èr bǎi qī shí sān)

1000 (一千 yī qiān) + 200 (二百 èr bǎi) + 70 (七十 qī shí) + 3 (三 sān)

EXAMPLE B3: 89,520

shí yì 十亿 Billion	yì 亿 Hundred Million	qiān wàn 千万 Ten Million	bǎi wàn 百万 Million	shí wàn 十万 Hundred Thousand	wàn 万 Ten Thousand	qiān 千 Thousand	bǎi 百 Hundred	shí 十 Ten	
					8 bā wàn 八万	9 jiǔ qiān 九千	5 wǔ bǎi 五百	2 èr shí 二十	0

89,520 = 八万九千五百二十 (bā wàn jiǔ qiān wǔ bǎi èr shí)

80,000 (八万 bā wàn) + 9000 (九千 jiǔ qiān) + 500 (五百 wǔ bǎi) + 20 (二十 èr shí)

EXAMPLE B4: 794,000

shí yì 十亿	yì 亿	qiān wàn 千万	bǎi wàn 百万	shí wàn 十万	wàn 万	qiān 千	bǎi 百	shí 十
Billion	Hundred Million	Ten Million	Million	Hundred Thousand	Ten Thousand	Thousand	Hundred	Ten
				7	9	4	0	0	0
				qī shí 七十	jiǔ wàn 九万	sì qiān 四千		

$$794,000 = \overset{qī}{七}\,\overset{shí}{十}\,\overset{jiǔ}{九}\,\overset{wàn}{万}\,\overset{sì}{四}\,\overset{qiān}{千}$$

700,000 (七 十 万) + 90,000 (九 万) + 4,000 (四 千)

IMPORTANT NOTE: *You may have noticed that in Chinese when we count between ten thousand and up to one hundred million, we count in multiples of ten thousand (万 wàn). So we do not pronounce the 万 wàn for every unit in this example, instead we would we just say 79万 (七 十 九 万) for that part.*

EXAMPLE B5: 9,000,000

shí yì 十亿	yì 亿	qiān wàn 千万	bǎi wàn 百万	shí wàn 十万	wàn 万	qiān 千	bǎi 百	shí 十
Billion	Hundred Million	Ten Million	Million	Hundred Thousand	Ten Thousand	Thousand	Hundred	Ten
			9	0	0	0	0	0	0
			jiǔ bǎi wàn 九百万					

$$9,000,000 = \overset{jiǔ}{九}\,\overset{bǎi}{百}\,\overset{wàn}{万}$$

EXAMPLE B6: 15,360,000

		wàn 万							
shí yì 十亿	yì 亿	qiān wàn 千万	bǎi wàn 百万	shí wàn 十万	wàn 万	qiān 千	bǎi 百	shí 十	
Billion	Hundred Million	Ten Million	Million	Hundred Thousand	Ten Thousand	Thousand	Hundred	Ten	
1	5	3	6	0	0	0	0		0
		yī qiān 一千	wǔ bǎi 五百	sān shí 三十	liù wàn 六万				

$$15{,}360{,}000 = \overset{\text{yī}}{-}\ \overset{\text{qiān}}{千}\ \overset{\text{wǔ}}{五}\ \overset{\text{bǎi}}{百}\ \overset{\text{sān}}{三}\ \overset{\text{shí}}{十}\ \overset{\text{liù}}{六}\ \overset{\text{wàn}}{万}$$

10,000,000 (一 千 万) + 5,000,000 (五 百 万)

+ 300,000 (三 十 万) + 60,000 (六 万)

You only need to pronounce 万 *once here:* 1536 万 (一 千 五 百 三 十 六 万).

EXAMPLE B7: 2,400,000,000

	yì 亿								
shí yì 十亿	yì 亿	qiān wàn 千万	bǎi wàn 百万	shí wàn 十万	wàn 万	qiān 千	bǎi 百	shí 十	
Billion	Hundred Million	Ten Million	Million	Hundred Thousand	Ten Thousand	Thousand	Hundred	Ten	
2	4	0	0	0	0	0	0	0	0
èr shí 二十	sì yì 四亿								

$$2{,}400{,}000{,}000 = \overset{\text{èr}}{二}\ \overset{\text{shí}}{十}\ \overset{\text{sì}}{四}\ \overset{\text{yì}}{亿}$$

2,000,000,000 (二十亿) + 400,000,000 (四亿)

Billions are also pronounced as multiples of one hundred million, so rather than repeating 亿 *for the billion and hundred million unit, we only say it once:* 24 亿 (二 十 四 亿).
This applies up to a trillion (兆 *).*

EXAMPLE B8: 1,761,829,400

yì 亿					wàn 万				
shí yì 十亿	yì 亿	qiān wàn 千万	bǎi wàn 百万	shí wàn 十万	wàn 万	qiān 千	bǎi 百	shí 十	
Billion	Hundred Million	Ten Million	Million	Hundred Thousand	Ten Thousand	Thousand	Hundred	Ten	
1	7	6	1	8	2	9	4	0	0
shí 十	qī yì 七亿	liù qiān 六千	yī bǎi 一百	bā shí 八十	èr wàn 二万	jiǔ qiān 九千	sì bǎi 四百		

1,761,829,400 = 十 七 亿 六 千 一 百 八 十 二 万 九 千 四 百
(shí qī yì liù qiān yī bǎi bā shí èr wàn jiǔ qiān sì bǎi)

1,700,000,000 (十 七 亿 shí qī yì) + 61,820,000 (六 千 一 百 八 十 二 万 liù qiān yī bǎi bā shí èr wàn)

+ 9000 (九 千 jiǔ qiān) + 400 (四 百 sì bǎi)

For the curious or mathemtically inclined among you, here are some even bigger units:

百 亿 (bǎi yì)   Ten Billion   X0,000,000,000

千 亿 (qiān yì)   Hundred Billion   X00,000,000,000

兆 (zhào)   Trillion   X,000,000,000,000

THE RULE OF ZERO

Whenever a number contains one or more zeros in-between other non-zero numbers, you need to say the zero out loud, but you only need to **say it once** for each series of zeros:

101   一 百 零 一 (yī bǎi líng yī)

909   九 百 零 九 (jiǔ bǎi líng jiǔ)

1002   一 千 零 二 (yī qiān líng èr)

10,006   一 万 零 六 (yī wàn líng liù)

100,703   十 万 零 七 百 零 三 (shí wàn líng qī bǎi líng sān)

THE RULE OF 10 TO 19

For numbers 10 to 19, the number 10 is simply read as 十 (shí) not 一十 (yī shí).

However, for numbers after 100 that end with any number between 10 - 19, you must add 一 (yī) in front of 十 (shí), to become 一十 (yī shí).

110 =	一 百 一 十 (yī bǎi yī shí)	**NOT** 一 百 十 (yī bǎi shí)
111 =	一 百 一 十 一 (yī bǎi yī shí yī)	**NOT** 一 百 十 一 (yī bǎi shí yī)
1112 =	一 千 一 百 一 十 二 (yī qiān yī bǎi yī shí èr)	**NOT** 一 千 一 百 十 二 (yī qiān yī bǎi shí èr)
11,113 =	一 万 一 千 一 百 一 十 三 (yī wàn yī qiān yī bǎi yī shí sān)	**NOT** 一 万 一 千 一 百 十 三 (yī wàn yī qiān yī bǎi shí sān)

SUMMARY

1. Master numbers zero to ten
2. Learn the "Non-10s Rule"
3. Learn the "10s Rule"
4. Master the bigger units names (100 - 1,000,000,000)
5. Learn the "Rule of Zero"
6. Learn the "Rule of 10 to 19"

WRITING NUMBERS IN CHINESE

In modern China, arabic numerals (0 to 9) are used widely when writing numbers, so don't worry too much about writing numbers using Chinese characters, you mostly need them to help with the pronunciation.

Another thing to note is that sometimes you will also see the number 0 written as ○. Most commonly used when writing years, for example the year 2025:

èr	líng	èr	wǔ	nián
二	○	二	五	年
2	0	2	5	year

Read digit by digit, not as a single number, when reading a year.

2

VOCABULARY IN CONTEXT

500 ESSENTIAL WORDS WITH EXAMPLES

FOR NEW HSK LEVEL 1

1 爱　　　　ài
Verb: to love
Noun: love

Verb
wǒ hěn ài mā ma
我 很 爱 妈 妈 。
I **love** mum very much.

Noun
wǒ duì tā de ài hěn shēn
我 对 她 的 爱 很 深 。
My **love** for her is very deep.

2 爱好　　　　ài hào
Noun: hobby

wǒ de ài hào shì qí chē
我 的 爱 好 是 骑 车 。
My **hobby** is cycling.

3 八　　　　bā
Number: eight

tā yǒu bā gè ér zi
他 有 八 个 儿 子 。
He has **eight** sons.

4 爸爸　　　　bà ba
Noun: dad

wǒ de bà ba wǔ shí suì le
我 的 爸 爸 五 十 岁 了 。
My **dad** is 50 years old.

5 吧　　　　ba
Auxiliary: indicate a mild suggestion

wǒ men yī qǐ chī fàn ba
我 们 一 起 吃 饭 吧 。
Let's eat together.

6 白   bái   **Adjective: white**

wǒ xǐ huān bái yī fú
我 喜 欢 白 衣 服 。
I like **white** clothes.

7 白天   bái tiān   **Noun: daytime**

wǒ bái tiān shàng bān
我 白 天 上 班 。
I go to work in the **daytime**.

8 百   bǎi   **Number: hundred**

zhè shì yī bǎi yuán
这 是 一 百 元 。
This is one **hundred** yuan (CNY).

9 班   bān   **Noun: class; work**

wǒ men bān yǒu shí gè rén
我 们 班 有 十 个 人 。
Our **class** has ten people

wǒ jīn tiān bù shàng bān
我 今 天 不 上 班 。
I am not going to **work** today.

10 半   bàn   **Noun: half**

wǒ chī le bàn gè píng guǒ
我 吃 了 半 个 苹 果 。
I ate **half** an apple.

11 半年   bàn nián   **Noun: half a year**

^{wǒ} ^{xué} ^{zhōng} ^{wén} ^{bàn} ^{nián} ^{le}
我 学 中 文 半 年 了 。
I have studied Chinese for **half a year**.

12 半天   bàn tiān   **Noun: half a day**

^{wǒ} ^{děng} ^{tā} ^{bàn} ^{tiān} ^{le}
我 等 他 半 天 了 。
I waited for him for **half a day**.

13 帮   bāng   **Verb: to help**

^{tā} ^{bāng} ^{wǒ} ^{zuò} ^{fàn}
她 帮 我 做 饭 。
She **helps** me to cook.

14 帮忙   bāng máng   **Verb: to help** / **Noun: help**

Verb
^{wǒ} ^{yào} ^{qǐng} ^{tā} ^{bāng} ^{máng}
我 要 请 她 帮 忙 。
I want to ask her **to help**.

Noun
^{xiè} ^{xie} ^{nǐ} ^{de} ^{bāng} ^{máng}
谢 谢 你 的 帮 忙 。
Thank you for your **help**.

15 包   bāo   **Noun: bag** / **Verb: to wrap**

Noun
^{wǒ} ^{mǎi} ^{le} ^{yī} ^{gè} ^{bāo}
我 买 了 一 个 包 。
I bought a **bag**.

Verb
^{wǒ} ^{yào} ^{bāo} ^{jiǎo} ^{zi}
我 要 包 饺 子 。
I want **to wrap** dumplings.

16 包子 bāo zi — Noun: steamed bun

wǒ chī le liǎng gè bāo zi
我 吃 了 两 个 包 子 。

I ate two **steamed buns**.

17 杯 bēi — Classifier: a cup of

wǒ hē le yī bēi kā fēi
我 喝 了 一 杯 咖 啡 。

I drank **a cup of** coffee.

18 杯子 bēi zi — Noun: cup

zhuō shàng yǒu gè lán sè de bēi zi
桌 上 有 个 蓝 色 的 杯 子 。

There is a blue **cup** on the table.

19 北 běi — Noun: north

tā gào sù wǒ men xiàng běi zǒu
他 告 诉 我 们 向 北 走 。

He told us to walk towards **north**.

20 北边 běi bian — Noun: north side

cháng chéng zài zhōng guó de běi bian
长 城 在 中 国 的 北 边 。

The Great Wall is on the **north side** of China.

21 北京 běi jīng — Noun: Beijing city

běi jīng shì zhōng guó de shǒu dōu
北 京 是 中 国 的 首 都 。

Beijing is the capital of China.

22 本　　　　　　　　běn　　　　**Classifer: for books; volumes**

^{wǒ}我 ^{mǎi}买 ^{le}了 ^{yī}一 ^{běn}**本** ^{shū}书 。

I bought a book.

23 本子　　　　　　běn zi　　　　**Noun: notebook**

^{zhè}这 ^{shì}是 ^{wǒ}我 ^{de}的 ^{xīn}新 ^{běn}**本** ^{zi}**子** 。

This is my new **notebook**.

24 比　　　　　　　bǐ　　　　　**Verb: to compare**

^{wǒ}我 ^{de}的 ^{gē}哥 ^{ge}哥 ^{bǐ}**比** ^{wǒ}我 ^{gāo}高 。

My older brother is taller **than** me.

25 别　　　　　　　bié　　　　　**Adverb: don't; not to**

^{bié}**别** ^{wàng}忘 ^{le}了 ^{dài}带 ^{qián}钱 ^{bāo}包 。

Don't forget to bring the wallet.

26 别的　　　　　　bié de　　　　**Noun: other**

^{wǒ}我 ^{méi}没 ^{yǒu}有 ^{mǎi}买 ^{bié}**别** ^{de}**的** ^{bǐ}笔 。

I didn't buy **other** pens.

27 别人　　　　　　bié rén　　　　**Noun: other people**

^{tā}他 ^{bù}不 ^{zài}在 ^{hū}乎 ^{bié}**别** ^{rén}**人** ^{de}的 ^{gǎn}感 ^{shòu}受 。

He doesn't care **other people**'s feelings.

28 病　　bìng　　**Verb: to get ill**
Noun: illness

Verb
他 病 了 ， 在 家 休 息 。
tā bìng le zài jiā xiū xi
He **got ill**, and is resting at home.

Noun
他 的 病 好 了 。
tā de bìng hǎo le
He (his **illness**) is recovered.

29 病人　　bìng rén　　**Noun: patient**

最 近 ，医 院 有 很 多 病 人 。
zuì jìn yī yuàn yǒu hěn duō bìng rén
Recently, the hospital has many **patients**.

30 不大　　bù dà　　**Adjective: not big**
Adverb: not often

Adj.
我 的 房 间 不 大 。
wǒ de fáng jiān bù dà
My room is **not big**.

Adv.
我 不 大 吃 鱼 。
wǒ bù dà chī yú
I **don't often** eat fish.

31 不对　　bù duì　　**Adjective: wrong**
(not right)

你 这 样 做 不 对 。
nǐ zhè yàng zuò bù duì
You are **not right** doing this (you shouldn't be doing this).

32 不客气　　bù kè qì　　**Phrase: you are**
welcome

他 对 我 说 ："不 客 气 "。
tā duì wǒ shuō bù kè qì
He said to me: "**You're welcome**".

33 不用   bù yòng   **Adverb: no need**

jīn wǎn bù yòng zuò fàn
今 晚 不 用 做 饭 。
No need to cook tonight.

34 不   bù   **Adverb: no; not**

wǒ bù shì měi guó rén
我 不 是 美 国 人 。
I am **not** American.

35 菜   cài   **Noun: dish**

wǒ xǐ huān chī zhōng guó cài
我 喜 欢 吃 中 国 菜 。
I like eating Chinese **dishes**.

36 茶   chá   **Noun: tea**

wǒ tiān tiān hē lǜ chá
我 天 天 喝 绿 茶 。
I drink green **tea** every day.

37a 差   chà   **Verb: less; short of**

chà wǔ fēn shí diǎn
差 五 分 十 点 。
It's 5 minutes to (**short of**) 10.

37b 差   chā   **Adjective: bad**

tā de zuò yè bù chā
他 的 作 业 不 差 。
His homework is not **bad**.

38 常   cháng   Adjective: ordinary

tā bù shì cháng rén
他 不 是 常 人 。
He is not an **ordinary** person.

39 常常   cháng cháng   Adverb: often

wǒ cháng cháng hē kā fēi
我 常 常 喝 咖 啡 。
I **often** drink coffee.

40 唱   chàng   Verb: to sing

nǐ huì chàng zhè shǒu gē ma
你 会 唱 这 首 歌 吗 ?
Can you **sing** this song?

41 唱歌   chàng gē   Verb: to sing (song)

wǒ hěn xǐ huān chàng gē
我 很 喜 欢 唱 歌 。
I like **singing** very much.

42 车   chē   Noun: car; vehicle

wǒ yǒu yī liàng hēi sè de chē
我 有 一 辆 黑 色 的 车 。
I have a black **car**.

43 车票   chē piào   Noun: tickets (transport)

wǒ yào mǎi liǎng zhāng chē piào
我 要 买 两 张 车 票 。
I want to buy 2 **tickets**.

44 车上   chē shàng   **Noun: on the vehicle**

chē shàng yǒu èr shí gè rén
车 上 有 二 十 个 人 。

There are 20 people **on the bus**.

45 车站   chē zhàn   **Noun: station**

wǒ zài huǒ chē zhàn děng nǐ
我 在 火 车 站 等 你 。

I am waiting for you at the **train station**.

46 吃   chī   **Verb: to eat**

wǒ xiǎng chī yī gè píng guǒ
我 想 吃 一 个 苹 果 。

I want to **eat** an apple.

47 吃饭   chī fàn   **Verb: have a meal**

wǒ men wǎn shàng qī diǎn chī fàn
我 们 晚 上 七 点 吃 饭 。

We will **have a meal** at 7pm.

48 出   chū   **Verb: out**

qǐng ná chū nǐ de hù zhào
请 拿 出 你 的 护 照 。

Please take **out** your passport.

49 出来   chū lái   **Verb: to come out**

tā cóng fàn guǎn chū lái le
她 从 饭 馆 出 来 了 。

She **came out** from the restaurant.

50 出去　chū qù　**Verb: to go out**

今 天 下 雨 , 我 不 想 出 去 。
jīn tiān xià yǔ wǒ bù xiǎng chū qù

It's raining today, I don't want to **go out**.

51 穿　chuān　**Verb: to wear**

他 常 常 穿 白 色 的 衬 衫 。
tā cháng cháng chuān bái sè de chèn shān

He often **wears** white shirts.

52 床　chuáng　**Noun: bed**

我 要 买 一 张 双 人 床 。
wǒ yào mǎi yī zhāng shuāng rén chuáng

I want to buy a double **bed**.

53 次　cì　**Classifer: position in series**

我 去 过 中 国 两 次 。
wǒ qù guò zhōng guó liǎng cì

I've been to China two **times**.

54 从　cóng　**Preposition: from**

我 从 香 港 坐 飞 机 到 北 京 。
wǒ cóng xiāng gǎng zuò fēi jī dào běi jīng

I took an airplane **from** Hong Kong to Beijing.

55 错　cuò　**Adjective: wrong**

对 不 起 , 我 记 错 时 间 了 。
duì bù qǐ wǒ jì cuò shí jiān le

Sorry, I remembered the time **wrong**.

56 打   dǎ   **Verb: to hit; beat**

tā zuó wǎn zài jiǔ ba bèi dǎ le
他 昨 晚 在 酒 吧 被 打 了 。
He got **beaten up** at the pub last night.

57 打车   dǎ chē   **Verb: to take a taxi**

nǐ kě yǐ zài fēi jī chǎng dǎ chē
你 可 以 在 飞 机 场 打 车 。
You can **take a taxi** at the airport.

58 打电话   dǎ diàn huà   **Verb: to make a call**

wǒ měi zhōu liù gěi mā ma dǎ diàn huà
我 每 周 六 给 妈 妈 打 电 话 。
I **call** mum every Saturday.

59 打开   dǎ kāi   **Verb: to open**

qǐng bù yào dǎ kāi zhè gè bāo guǒ
请 不 要 打 开 这 个 包 裹 。
Please don't **open** this parcel.

60 打球   dǎ qiú   **Verb: to play ball**

wǒ men qù cāo chǎng dǎ qiú hǎo ma
我 们 去 操 场 打 球 , 好 吗 ?
Let's go to the playground to **play ball**, OK?

61 大   dà   **Adjective: big**

wǒ shū shu jiā de huā yuán hěn dà
我 叔 叔 家 的 花 园 很 大 。
The garden in my uncle's house is very **big**.

62 大学
dà xué

Noun: university

这 个 大学 很 有 名 。
zhè gè dà xué hěn yǒu míng

This **university** is very famous.

63 大学生
dà xué shēng

Noun: university student

我 的 姐 姐 是 大学 生 。
wǒ de jiě jie shì dà xué shēng

My older sister is a **university student**.

64 到
dào

Verb: to arrive

他 昨 天 到 上 海 。
tā zuó tiān dào shàng hǎi

He **arrived** in Shanghai yesterday.

65 得到
dé dào

Verb: to obtain

我 想 得 到 爸 爸 的 支 持 。
wǒ xiǎng dé dào bà ba de zhī chí

I want to **obtain** dad's support.

66 地
de

structural particle

他 努 力 地 学 习 中 文 。
tā nǔ lì de xué xí zhōng wén

He studies Chinese very hard.

67 的
de

possessive particle

我 的 狗 很 可 爱 。
wǒ de gǒu hěn kě ài

My dog is very cute.

68 等   děng   **Verb: to wait**

wǒ liù diǎn zài shì zhōng xīn děng nǐ
我 六 点 在 市 中 心 等 你 。
I will **wait** for you in city centre at 6pm.

69 地   dì   **Noun: land**

wǒ zài nóng cūn mǎi le yī kuài dì
我 在 农 村 买 了 一 块 地 。
I bought a piece of **land** in the countryside.

70 地点   dì diǎn   **Noun: location**

qǐng wèn kāi huì dì diǎn zài nǎ
请 问 , 开 会 地 点 在 哪 ?
May I ask, where is the **location** for the meeting?

71 地方   dì fang   **Noun: place**

zhè gè dì fang de rén men hěn yǒu hǎo
这 个 地 方 的 人 们 很 友 好 。
People in this **place** are very friendly.

72 地上   dì shàng   **Noun: ground**

dì shàng yǒu wǔ zhǐ māo
地 上 有 五 只 猫 。
There are 5 cats on the **ground**.

73 地图   dì tú   **Noun: map**

wǒ yào mǎi yī zhāng cháng chéng de dì tú
我 要 买 一 张 长 城 的 地 图 。
I want to buy a **map** of the Great Wall.

74 弟弟   dì di   Noun: younger brother

wǒ de dì di shì zú qiú yùn dòng yuán
我 的 弟 弟 是 足 球 运 动 员 。
My **younger brother** is a football player.

75 第   dì   Prefix: to form ordinal number

zhè shì wǒ dì yī cì qù zhōng guó
这 是 我 第 一 次 去 中 国 。
This is my **first** time to go to China.

76 点   diǎn   Noun: drop; point Verb: to order

Noun
yè zi shàng yǒu yǔ diǎn
叶 子 上 有 雨 点 。
There are rain**drops** on the leaves.

Verb
wǒ yào diǎn zhōng cān wài mài
我 要 点 中 餐 外 卖 。
I want to **order** Chinese takeaway.

77 电   diàn   Noun: electricity; battery

wǒ de shǒu jī méi diàn le
我 的 手 机 没 电 了 。
My phone has run out of **battery**.

78 电话   diàn huà   Noun: telephone

qǐng wèn nǐ de diàn huà hào mǎ shì duō shǎo
请 问 , 你 的 电 话 号 码 是 多 少 ?
May I ask, what's your **telephone** number?

79 电脑   diàn nǎo   **Noun: computer**

wǒ mǎi le yī tái xīn diàn nǎo
我 买 了 一 台 新 **电 脑** 。
I bought a new **computer**.

80 电视   diàn shì   **Noun: TV (show)**

wǒ měi tiān wǎn shàng bā diǎn kàn diàn shì
我 每 天 晚 上 八 点 看 **电 视** 。
I watch **TV** every night at 8 o'clock.

81 电视机   diàn shì jī   **Noun: TV set**

wǒ jiā de diàn shì jī huài le
我 家 的 **电 视 机** 坏 了 。
The **TV set** in my house is broken.

82 电影   diàn yǐng   **Noun: movie**

wǒ jīn wǎn huì gēn péng yǒu yī qǐ kàn diàn yǐng
我 今 晚 会 跟 朋 友 一 起 看 **电 影** 。
I will watch a **movie** with my friends tonight.

83 电影院   diàn yǐng yuàn   **Noun: cinema**

shì zhōng xīn yǒu sān gè diàn yǐng yuàn
市 中 心 有 三 个 **电 影 院** 。
There are three **cinemas** in the city center.

84 东   dōng   **Noun: east**

tā gào sù wǒ yào wǎng dōng zǒu
他 告 诉 我 要 往 **东** 走 。
He told me to walk towards **east**.

85 东边 — dōng bian — **Noun: east side**

wǒ jiā zài lún dūn de dōng bian
我 家 在 伦 敦 的 东 边 。

My home is on the **east side** of London.

86 东西 — dōng xi — **Noun: things; stuff**

wǒ xiàn zài qù shāng diàn mǎi dōng xi
我 现 在 去 商 店 买 东 西 。

I am going to the shop to buy **things** now.

87 动 — dòng — **Verb: to move**

jǐng chá ràng xiǎo tōu bié dòng
警 察 让 小 偷 别 动 。

The policeman asked the thief not to **move**.

88 动作 — dòng zuò — **Noun: move; action**

qǐng jiāo wǒ zuò zhè gè dòng zuò
请 教 我 做 这 个 动 作 。

Please teach me to do this **move**.

89 都 — dōu — **Adverb: both; all**

wǒ men dōu fēi cháng xǐ huān gǒu
我 们 都 非 常 喜 欢 狗 。

We **both** like dogs very much.

90 读 — dú — **Verb: to read**

lǎo shī ràng wǒ men dú zhōng wén gù shì
老 师 让 我 们 读 中 文 故 事 。

The teacher asks us to **read** Chinese stories.

91 读书　dú shū — Verb: to study; to attend school

他 读书 很 努力。
tā dú shū hěn nǔ lì
He **studies** very hard.

我 妹妹 今年 十三 岁，在 读书。
wǒ mèi mei jīn nián shí sān suì zài dú shū
My younger sister is 13-year-old, and is **attending school**.

92 对　duì — Adjective: correct / Preposition: regarding

Adj
他 的 回答 很 对。
tā de huí dá hěn duì
His answer is very **correct**.

Pre.
对 这 件 事，我们 有 不同 的 看法。
duì zhè jiàn shì wǒ men yǒu bù tóng de kàn fǎ
Regarding this matter, we have different views.

93 对不起　duì bù qǐ — Phrase: sorry

我 觉得 非常 对不起。
wǒ jué dé fēi cháng duì bù qǐ
I feel very **sorry**.

94 多　duō — Adjective: many

我 买 了 很 多 苹果。
wǒ mǎi le hěn duō píng guǒ
I bought **many** apples.

95 多少　duō shǎo — Pronoun: how much; how many

这 台 电脑 多少 钱？
zhè tái diàn nǎo duō shǎo qián
How much (money) is this computer?

nǐ men gōng sī yǒu duō shǎo rén
你 们 公 司 有 多 少 人 ？
How many people does your company have?

96 饿　　　　　è　　　　　Adjective: hungry

wǒ jué dé hěn è xiǎng chī fàn
我 觉 得 很 饿 ，想 吃 饭 。
I feel very **hungry** and want to eat.

97 儿子　　　　ér zi　　　　Noun: son

tā ér zi zài shàng dà xué
他 儿 子 在 上 大 学 。
His **son** is attending university.

98 二　　　　　è r　　　　Number: two; second

wǒ men zhù zài è r lóu
我 们 住 在 二 楼 。
We live on the **second** floor.

99 饭　　　　　fàn　　　　Noun: meal; rice

wǒ yào dài nǚ péng yǒu qù chī fàn
我 要 带 女 朋 友 去 吃 饭 。
I want to bring my girlfriend to have a **meal**.

wǒ men dōu hěn xǐ huān chī mǐ fàn
我 们 都 很 喜 欢 吃 米 饭 。
We all like to eat **rice**.

100 饭店　　　　fàn diàn　　　Noun: restaurant; hotel

wǒ nán péng yǒu zài fàn diàn děng wǒ
我 男 朋 友 在 饭 店 等 我 。
My boyfriend is waiting for me at the **restaurant**.

101 房间   fáng jiān   **Noun: room**

wǒ fù mǔ jiā yǒu wǔ gè fáng jiān
我 父 母 家 有 五 个 房 间 。
My parents' house has five **rooms**.

102 房子   fáng zi   **Noun: house**

wǒ qù nián mǎi le yī tào xīn fáng zi
我 去 年 买 了 一 套 新 房 子 。
I bought a new **house** last year.

103 放   fàng   **Verb: to release**

wǒ men bù néng fàng zhè gè xiǎo tōu
我 们 不 能 放 这 个 小 偷 。
We cannot **release** this thief.

104 放假   fàng jià   **Verb: to have holiday**

zài shèng dàn jié wǒ men huì fàng jià sān tiān
在 圣 诞 节 ，我 们 会 放 假 三 天 。
On Christmas, we will **have** a three-day **holiday**.

105 放学   fàng xué   **Verb: to finish school**

wǒ men xià wǔ sān diǎn bàn fàng xué
我 们 下 午 三 点 半 放 学 。
We **finish school** at 3:30 in the afternoon.

106 飞   fēi   **Verb: to fly**

xiǎo niǎo men zài tiān shàng fēi
小 鸟 们 在 天 上 飞 。
Birds are **flying** in the sky.

107 飞机   fēi jī   **Noun: airplane**

wǒ huì wǎn shàng bā diǎn shàng fēi jī
我 会 晚 上 八 点 上 飞 机 。

I will board the **airplane** at 8 o'clock in the evening.

108 非常   fēi cháng   **Adverb: extremely**

zhè gè nǚ shēng fēi cháng piào liàng
这 个 女 生 非 常 漂 亮 。

This girl is **extremely** beautiful.

109 分   fēn   **Noun: minutes**
Verb: to divide

Noun

xiàn zài shì jiǔ diǎn líng wǔ fēn
现 在 是 九 点 零 五 分 。

Now the time is five **minutes** past nine (9:05).

Verb

tā zài gěi wǒ men fēn dàn gāo
她 在 给 我 们 分 蛋 糕 。

She is **dividing** the cake for us.

110 风   fēng   **Noun: wind**

zuó tiān hǎi biān guā dà fēng
昨 天 海 边 刮 大 风 。

Yesterday there was big **wind** at the seaside.

111 干   gān   **Adjective: dry**

zuì jìn tiān qì hěn gān
最 近 , 天 气 很 干 。

Recently, the weather has been very **dry**.

112 干净　　　gān jìng　　　**Adjective: clean**

他 们 的 客 厅 很 干 净 。
tā men de kè tīng hěn gān jìng

Their living room is very **clean**.

113 干　　　gàn　　　**Verb: do (colloquial)**

你 在 干 吗 ？
nǐ zài gàn ma

What are you **doing**?

114 干什么　　　gàn shénme　　　**Phrase: up to what (colloquial)**

你 们 想 干 什 么 ？
nǐ men xiǎng gàn shén me

What are you guys **up to**?

115 高　　　gāo　　　**Adjective: high; tall**

这 座 教 堂 很 高 。
zhè zuò jiào táng hěn gāo

This church is very **tall**.

116 高兴　　　gāo xìng　　　**Adjective: happy**

今 天 是 我 的 生 日 ， 我 很 高 兴 。
jīn tiān shì wǒ de shēng rì wǒ hěn gāo xīng

Today is my birthday, I am very **happy**.

117 告诉　　　gào sù　　　**Verb: to tell**

他 告 诉 了 我 一 个 好 消 息 。
tā gào sù le wǒ yī gè hǎo xiāo xī

He **told** me a good news.

118 哥哥   gē ge   **Noun: older brother**

wǒ de gē ge shì yī míng fēi xíng yuán
我 的 哥 哥 是 一 名 飞 行 员 。

My **older brother** is a pilot.

119 歌   gē   **Noun: song**

wǒ xǐ huān tīng liú xíng gē
我 喜 欢 听 流 行 歌 。

I like listening to pop **songs**.

120 个   gè   **Classifier: a; an**

wǒ zuò le yī gè píng guǒ bǐng
我 做 了 一 个 苹 果 饼 。

I made **an** apple pie.

121 给   gěi   **Verb: to give**

qǐng gěi wǒ yī bēi shuǐ
请 给 我 一 杯 水 。

Please **give** me a cup of water.

122 跟   gēn   **Verb: with**

wǒ huì gēn péng yǒu qù fǎ guó lǚ yóu
我 会 跟 朋 友 去 法 国 旅 游 。

I will travel to France **with** my friend.

123 工人   gōng rén   **Noun: worker**

zhè jiā gōng chǎng yǒu liǎng bǎi gè gōng rén
这 家 工 厂 有 两 百 个 工 人 。

This factory has two hundred **workers**.

124 工作　gōng zuò　**Verb: to work**
Noun: job

Verb
tā zài niǔ yuē gōng zuò
他 在 纽 约 工 作 。
He **works** in New York.

Noun
kě shì tā bù xǐ huān tā de gōng zuò
可 是 , 他 不 喜 欢 他 的 工 作 。
But, he doesn't like his **job**.

125 关　guān　**Verb: to shut; turn off**

fēi jī yào qǐ fēi le qǐng guān shǒu jī
飞 机 要 起 飞 了 , 请 关 手 机 。
The plane is about to take off, please **turn off** your phone.

126 关上　guān shàng　**Verb: to close**

qǐng nǐ guān shàng mén
请 你 关 上 门 。
Please **close** the door.

127 贵　guì　**Adjective: expensive**

zuì xīn de píng guǒ shǒu jī hěn guì
最 新 的 苹 果 手 机 很 贵 。
The latest iPhone (apple phone) is very **expensive**.

128 国　guó　**Noun: country**

wǒ qù guò zhōng guó yīng guó hé měi guó
我 去 过 中 国 、 英 国 和 美 国 。
I've been to China, the UK and the US.

129 国家　　guó jiā　　**Noun: nation; homeland**

wǒ hěn ài wǒ de guó jiā
我 很 爱 我 的 国 家 。
I love my **homeland** very much.

130 国外　　guó wài　　**Noun: overseas; abroad**

wǒ de ā yí zhù zài guó wài
我 的 阿 姨 住 在 国 外 。
My aunt lives **abroad**.

131 过　　guò　　**Verb: to cross; to have**

wǒ yào guò mǎ lù
我 要 过 马 路 。
I want to **cross** the road

wǒ men zài èr yuè fèn guò chūn jié le
我 们 在 二 月 份 过 春 节 了 。
We **had** the Spring Festival in February

132 还　　hái　　**Adverb: also**

wǒ yào qù zhōng guó hái yào qù rì běn
我 要 去 中 国 ，还 要 去 日 本 。
I want to go to China, **also** want to go to Japan.

133 还是　　hái shì　　**Conjuction: or Adverb: still**

Conj.
nǐ yào hē kā fēi hái shì yào hē chá
你 要 喝 咖 啡 ，还 是 要 喝 茶 ？
You want to drink coffee **or** tea?

Adv.
tā hái shì bù zhī dào wǒ ài tā
她 还 是 不 知 道 我 爱 她 。
She **still** doesn't know that I love her.

134 还有   hái yǒu   **Adverb: also; additionally**

wǒ yǒu yī gè gē ge hái yǒu liǎng gè dì di
我 有 一 个 哥 哥 , 还 有 两 个 弟 弟 。

I have one older brother, **also** two younger brothers.

135 孩子   hái zi   **Noun: child; children**

wǒ sòng hái zi qù yòu ér yuán
我 送 孩 子 去 幼 儿 园 。

I am sending my **child** to nursery.

136 汉语   hàn yǔ   **Noun: Mandarin**

wǒ huì shuō hàn yǔ hé yīng yǔ
我 会 说 汉 语 和 英 语 。

I can speak **Mandarin** and English.

137 汉字   hàn zì   **Noun: Chinese characters**

lǎo shī ràng wǒ liàn xí xiě hàn zì
老 师 让 我 练 习 写 汉 字 。

Teacher asked me to practice writing **Chinese characters**.

138 好   hǎo   **Adjective: good; OK**

tā men dōu shì wǒ de hǎo péng yǒu
他 们 都 是 我 的 好 朋 友 。

They are all my **good** friends.

wǒ men yī qǐ qù chī wǎn fàn hǎo ma
我 们 一 起 去 吃 晚 饭 , 好 吗 ?

Let's go to have dinner together, **OK**?

139 好吃   hǎo chī   **Adjective: delicious**

mā ma zuò de fàn cài hěn hǎo chī
妈 妈 做 的 饭 菜 很 好 吃 。

The food my mum cooks is very **delicious**.

140 好看   hǎo kàn   **Adjective: good-looking**

zhè gè xiǎo huǒ zi zhǎng dé hěn hǎo kàn
这 个 小 伙 子 长 得 很 好 看 。

This young man is very **good-looking**.

141 好听   hǎo tīng   **Adjective: pleasant to hear**

zhè shǒu zhōng wén gē hěn hǎo tīng
这 首 中 文 歌 很 好 听 。

This Chinese song is very **pleasant (to hear)**.

142 好玩   hǎo wán   **Adjective: fun**

dǎ wǎng qiú hěn hǎo wán
打 网 球 很 好 玩 。

Playing tennis is very **fun**.

143 号   hào   **ordinal**

wǒ de shēng rì shì yī jiǔ jiǔ wǔ nián shí yuè yī hào
我 的 生 日 是 一 九 九 五 年 十 月 一 号 。

My birthday was October 1st, 1995.

144 喝   hē   **Verb: to drink**

tā zuì xǐ huān hē hóng chá
他 最 喜 欢 喝 红 茶 。

He likes **drinking** red tea the most.

145 和　　　hé　　　**Conjuction: and; with**

bà ba hé wǒ míng tiān yī qǐ qù chá guǎn
爸 爸 和 我 明 天 一 起 去 茶 馆 。
Dad **and** I will go to the tea house tomorrow together.

146 很　　　hěn　　　**Adverb: very**

tā hěn piào liàng yě hěn cōng míng
她 很 漂 亮 , 也 很 聪 明 。
She is **very** beautiful, and **very** smart.

147 后　　　hòu　　　**Noun: after**

tā men jié hūn hòu jiù yī qǐ zhù zài běi jīng
他 们 结 婚 后 , 就 一 起 住 在 北 京 。
After they married, they lived in Beijing together.

148 后边　　　hòu biān　　　**Noun: behind**

zhè zuò shān de hòu biān shì dà hǎi
这 座 山 的 后 边 是 大 海 。
Behind this mountain is the sea.

149 后天　　　hòu tiān　　　**Noun: the day after tomorrow**

hòu tiān wǒ men huì qù pá shān
后 天 我 们 会 去 爬 山 。
We will go to climb the mountain **the day after tomorrow**.

150 花　huā

Noun: flower
Verb: to spend

Noun

chūn tiān de shí hòu, hěn duō huā kāi le
春 天 的 时 候 , 很 多 花 开 了 。
In spring, many **flowers** bloom.

Verb

tā huā le hěn duō qián xué huá xuě
他 花 了 很 多 钱 学 滑 雪 。
He **spent** lots of money to learn to ski.

151 话　huà

Noun: words; talk

tā de huà ràng wǒ jué dé hěn gāo xìng
他 的 话 让 我 觉 得 很 高 兴 。
His **words** make me feel very happy.

152 坏　huài

Adjective: broken; bad

wǒ de shǒu jī huài le
我 的 手 机 坏 了 。
My phone is **broken**.

xiǎo xīn, tā kě néng shì huài rén
小 心 , 他 可 能 是 坏 人 。
Be careful, he might be a **bad** man.

153 还　hái

Adverb: yet; still

wǒ men hái méi yǒu kāi shǐ yuē huì
我 们 还 没 有 开 始 约 会 。
We haven't started to date **yet**.

154 回　huí

Verb: to return to

tā men xià gè yuè huí měi guó
他 们 下 个 月 回 美 国 。
They will **return to** the US next month.

41

155 回答   huí dá   **Verb: to answer**

qǐng nǐ huí dá wǒ men de wèn tí
请 你 回 答 我 们 的 问 题 。
Please **answer** our questions.

156 回到   huí dào   **Verb: to have returned**

wǒ gāng gāng huí dào shàng hǎi
我 刚 刚 回 到 上 海 。
I 've just **returned** to Shanghai.

157 回家   huí jiā   **Verb: go home**

mā ma dǎ diàn huà ràng wǒ huí jiā
妈 妈 打 电 话 让 我 回 家 。
Mum called to ask me to **go home**.

158 回来   huí lái   **Verb: come back**

wài miàn zài xià yǔ nǐ kuài huí lái
外 面 在 下 雨 , 你 快 回 来 。
It's raining outside, **come back** quickly.

159 回去   huí qù   **Verb: go back**

tài wǎn le wǒ děi huí qù
太 晚 了 , 我 得 回 去 。
It's too late, I need to **go back**.

160 会   huì   **Verb: can; will**

wǒ huì kāi chē
我 会 开 车 。
I **can** (know how to) drive .

wǒ míng tiān huì qù lún dūn
我 明 天 会 去 伦 敦 。
I **will** (plan to) go to London tomorrow.

161 火车 huǒ chē **Noun: train**

wǒ men yào zuò huǒ chē qù jiā xiāng
我 们 要 坐 火 车 去 家 乡 。
We are going to hometown by **train**.

162 机场 jī chǎng **Noun: airport**

bà bà huì kāi chē dào jī chǎng jiē wǒ
爸 爸 会 开 车 到 机 场 接 我 。
Dad will drive car to the **airport** to pick me up.

163 机票 jī piào **Noun: plane ticket**

nín hǎo wǒ yào mǎi yī zhāng qù xiāng gǎng de jī piào
您 好 ！ 我 要 买 一 张 去 香 港 的 机 票。
Hello! I want to buy a **plane ticket** to Hong Kong.

164 鸡蛋 jī dàn **Noun: egg**

wǒ mǎi le yī xiē jī dàn
我 买 了 一 些 鸡 蛋 。
I bought some **eggs**.

165 几 jǐ **a few; how many**

chú fáng yǒu jǐ gè xiāng jiāo
厨 房 有 几 个 香 蕉 。
There are **a few** bananas in the kitchen

nǐ jiā yǒu jǐ gè rén
你 家 有 几 个 人 ？
How many people are there in your family?

43

166 记　　　jì　　　**Verb: to take; record**

shàng kè de shí hòu wǒ huì jì bǐ jì
上 课 的 时 候 ，我 会 记 笔 记 。
During class, I will **take** notes.

167 记得　　　jì dé　　　**Verb: to remember**

wǒ bù jì dé tā duō shǎo suì
我 不 记 得 她 多 少 岁 。
I don't **remember** how old she is.

168 记住　　　jì zhù　　　**Verb: remember (learn)**

wǒ yào jì zhù zhè gè shēng cí
我 要 记 住 这 个 生 词 。
I need to **remember** this new word.

169 家　　　jiā　　　**Noun: home**

wǒ měi nián shèng dàn jié huí jiā
我 每 年 圣 诞 节 回 家 。
I go **home** every year on Christmas.

170 家里　　　jiā lǐ　　　**Noun: home (inside)**

yé ye hé nǎi nai bù zài jiā lǐ
爷 爷 和 奶 奶 不 在 家 里 。
Grandpa and grandma (paternal) are not at **home**.

171 家人　　　jiā rén　　　**Noun: family (members)**

wǒ de gǒu yě shì wǒ de jiā rén
我 的 狗 也 是 我 的 家 人 。
My dog is also my **family (member)**.

172 间   jiān   **Classifer for rooms**

gōng sī yǒu èr shí jiān bàn gōng shì
公 司 有 二 十 间 办 公 室 。
The company has 20 offices.

173 见   jiàn   **Verb: to see**

wǒ bù xiǎng jiàn tā
我 不 想 见 他 。
I dont want to **see** him.

174 见面   jiàn miàn   **Verb: to meet (up)**

wǒ men kě yǐ zài kā fēi guǎn jiàn miàn
我 们 可 以 在 咖 啡 馆 见 面 。
We can **meet up** at the coffee shop.

175 教   jiāo   **Verb: to teach; show**

mā ma jiāo wǒ zuò dàn gāo
妈 妈 教 我 做 蛋 糕 。
Mum **taught** me to make cakes.

176 叫   jiào   **Verb: to call; to scream**

nǐ kě yǐ jiào wǒ " dà wéi "
你 可 以 叫 我 " 大 为 " 。
You can **call** me "Dawei".

wǒ tīng dào hái zi zài jiào
我 听 到 孩 子 在 叫 。
I heard the child **screaming**.

177 教学楼   jiào xué lóu   **Noun: teaching building**

lǎo shī men zài jiào xué lóu kāi huì
老 师 们 在 教 学 楼 开 会 。
Teachers are having meetings in the **teaching building**.

178 姐姐   jiě jie   **older sister**

wǒ jiě jie shì yī wèi lǜ shī
我 姐 姐 是 一 位 律 师 。
My **older sister** is a lawyer.

179 介绍   jiè shào   **Verb: to introduce**

wǒ jiè shào yī xià zhè shì wǒ men de zǒng jīng lǐ
我 介 绍 一 下 , 这 是 我 们 的 总 经 理 。
Let me **introduce** a bit, this is our general manager.

180 今年   jīn nián   **Noun: this year**

wǒ jīn nián yào qù zhōng guó lǚ yóu
我 今 年 要 去 中 国 旅 游 。
I am going to travel to China **this year**.

181 今天   jīn tiān   **Noun: today**

jīn tiān shì wǒ tài tai de shēng rì
今 天 是 我 太 太 的 生 日 。
Today is my wife's birthday.

182 进   jìn   **Verb: to enter**

wǒ de māo bù kě yǐ jìn chú fáng
我 的 猫 不 可 以 进 厨 房 。
My cat cannot **enter** the kitchen

183 进来　jìn lái　**Verb: to come in**

<ruby>下<rt>xià</rt></ruby> <ruby>雨<rt>yǔ</rt></ruby> <ruby>了<rt>le</rt></ruby>，<ruby>你<rt>nǐ</rt></ruby> <ruby>们<rt>men</rt></ruby> <ruby>快<rt>kuài</rt></ruby> <ruby>点<rt>diǎn</rt></ruby> <ruby>进<rt>jìn</rt></ruby> <ruby>来<rt>lái</rt></ruby> 。

It's raining, **come in** quickly.

184 进去　jìn qù　**Verb: to go in**

<ruby>这<rt>zhè</rt></ruby> <ruby>是<rt>shì</rt></ruby> <ruby>总<rt>zǒng</rt></ruby> <ruby>统<rt>tǒng</rt></ruby> <ruby>办<rt>bàn</rt></ruby> <ruby>公<rt>gōng</rt></ruby> <ruby>室<rt>shì</rt></ruby>，<ruby>我<rt>wǒ</rt></ruby> <ruby>们<rt>men</rt></ruby> <ruby>不<rt>bù</rt></ruby> <ruby>能<rt>néng</rt></ruby> <ruby>进<rt>jìn</rt></ruby> <ruby>去<rt>qù</rt></ruby>。

This is the president's office, we cannot **go in**.

185 九　jiǔ　**Number: nine**

<ruby>我<rt>wǒ</rt></ruby> <ruby>去<rt>qù</rt></ruby> <ruby>超<rt>chāo</rt></ruby> <ruby>市<rt>shì</rt></ruby> <ruby>买<rt>mǎi</rt></ruby> <ruby>了<rt>le</rt></ruby> <ruby>九<rt>jiǔ</rt></ruby> <ruby>个<rt>gè</rt></ruby> <ruby>鸡<rt>jī</rt></ruby> <ruby>蛋<rt>dàn</rt></ruby> 。

I went to the supermarket and bought **9** eggs.

186 就　jiù　**Adverb: used to place emphasis**

<ruby>我<rt>wǒ</rt></ruby> <ruby>就<rt>jiù</rt></ruby> <ruby>是<rt>shì</rt></ruby> <ruby>不<rt>bù</rt></ruby> <ruby>知<rt>zhī</rt></ruby> <ruby>道<rt>dào</rt></ruby> 。

I **just** don't know.

187 觉得　jué dé　**Verb: to think; to feel**

<ruby>我<rt>wǒ</rt></ruby> <ruby>觉<rt>jué</rt></ruby> <ruby>得<rt>dé</rt></ruby> <ruby>肚<rt>dù</rt></ruby> <ruby>子<rt>zi</rt></ruby> <ruby>不<rt>bù</rt></ruby> <ruby>舒<rt>shū</rt></ruby> <ruby>服<rt>fú</rt></ruby> 。

I **feel** my stomach is uncomfortable.

188 开　kāi　**Verb: to open**

<ruby>您<rt>nín</rt></ruby> <ruby>好<rt>hǎo</rt></ruby> ！<ruby>请<rt>qǐng</rt></ruby> <ruby>开<rt>kāi</rt></ruby> <ruby>门<rt>mén</rt></ruby> 。

Hello! Please **open** the door.

189 开车   kāi chē   **Verb: to drive**

wǒ cháng cháng kāi chē qù bā lí
我 常 常 开 车 去 巴 黎 。
I often **drive** to Paris.

190 开会   kāi huì   **Verb: to have meeting**

wǒ jué dé kāi huì hěn wú liáo
我 觉 得 开 会 很 无 聊 。
I think **having meetings** is very boring.

191 开玩笑   kāi wán xiào   **Verb: to make jokes**

tā hěn yōu mò cháng cháng kāi wán xiào
他 很 幽 默 ， 常 常 开 玩 笑 。
He is very humorous and often **makes jokes**.

192 看   kàn   **Verb: to see; visit**

wǒ yào huí jiā xiāng kàn mā ma
我 要 回 家 乡 看 妈 妈 。
I am going back to hometown **to visit** my mum.

193 看病   kàn bìng   **Verb: to see doctor**

wǒ huì péi tā qù yī yuàn kàn bìng
我 会 陪 她 去 医 院 看 病 。
I will accompany her to the hospital to **see a doctor**.

194 看到   kàn dào   **Verb: to have seen; spotted**

wǒ zài hé lǐ kàn dào yī zhī tiān é
我 在 河 里 看 到 一 只 天 鹅 。
I've **spotted** a swan in the river.

195 看见　　kàn jiàn　　**Verb: to see; view**

tā de yǎn jīng huī fù le ， néng kàn jiàn le
她 的 眼 睛 恢 复 了 ， 能 看 见 了 。

Her eyes are recovered, and could **see**.

196 考　　kǎo　　**Verb: to test**

lǎo shī dǎ suàn kǎo yī xià wǒ
老 师 打 算 考 一 下 我 。

The teacher plans to **test** me a bit.

197 考试　　kǎo shì　　**Noun: exam**
Verb: to take exam

Noun
wǒ zuì hèn kǎo shì
我 最 恨 考 试 。

I hate **exams** the most.

Verb
wǒ xià zhōu èr yào kǎo shì
我 下 周 二 要 考 试 。

I will **take an exam** next Tuesday.

198 喝　　hē　　**Verb: to drink**

wǒ jué dé hěn kě ， xiǎng hē shuǐ
我 觉 得 很 渴 ， 想 喝 水 。

I feel very thirsty, and want to **drink** water.

199 课　　kè　　**Noun: lesson; class**

wǒ hěn xǐ huān lì shǐ kè
我 很 喜 欢 历 史 课 。

I like history **lessons** very much.

200 课本   kè běn   **Noun: textbook**

zhè běn zhōng wén kè běn hěn shí yòng
这 本 中 文 课 本 很 实 用 。

This Chinese **textbook** is very practical.

201 课文   kè wén   **Noun: lesson text**

lǎo shī ràng wǒ fù xí kè wén
老 师 让 我 复 习 课 文 。

The teacher asked me to review the **lesson text**.

202 口   kǒu   **Noun: mouth; opening area**

qǐng nǐ zhāng kǒu
请 你 张 口 。

Please open your **mouth**.

qǐng wèn dì tiě zhàn de rù kǒu zài nǎ
请 问 ，地 铁 站 的 入 口 在 哪 ？

Excuse me, where is the **entrance** of the subway station?

203 块   kuài   **Classifer: slice; piece**

wǒ chī le jǐ kuài dàn gāo
我 吃 了 几 块 蛋 糕 。

I ate a few **slices** of cake.

204 快   kuài   **Adjective: soon; fast**

tā de fēi jī kuài dào le ma
他 的 飞 机 快 到 了 吗 ？

Is his plane arriving **soon**?

zhè gè yùn dòng yuán pǎo dé hěn kuài
这 个 运 动 员 跑 得 很 快 。

The athlete runs very **fast**.

205 来　　lái　　**Verb: to come**

nín hǎo wǒ lái miàn shì
您 好 ！我 来 面 试 。
Hello! I **come** for the interview.

206 来到　　lái dào　　**Verb: to arrive**

chūn tiān zhōng yú lái dào le
春 天 终 于 来 到 了 ！
Spring has finally **arrived**!

207 老　　lǎo　　**Adjective: old**

wǒ de fù mǔ yǐ jīng lǎo le
我 的 父 母 已 经 老 了 。
My parents are already **old**.

208 老人　　lǎo rén　　**Noun: old person; elderly**

qǐng gěi lǎo rén ràng zuò
请 给 老 人 让 座 。
Please give your seats to the **elderly**.

209 老师　　lǎo shī　　**Noun: teacher**

wǒ men xué xiào yǒu yī bǎi gè lǎo shī
我 们 学 校 有 一 百 个 老 师 。
Our school has one hundred **teachers**.

210 了　　le　　**to indicate completion of action**

tā hé nǚ péng yǒu fēn shǒu le
他 和 女 朋 友 分 手 了 。
He broke up with his girlfriend.

51

211 累　　　lèi　　　**Adjective: tired**

我 工 作 了 一 天 ， 觉 得 很 累 。
wǒ gōng zuò le yī tiān， jué dé hěn lèi

I worked for a day, and feel very **tired**.

212 冷　　　lěng　　　**Adjective: cold**

下 雪 的 时 候 ， 我 觉 得 很 冷 。
xià xuě de shí hòu， wǒ jué dé hěn lěng

When it snows, I feel very **cold**.

213 里　　　lǐ　　　**Noun: in; inside**

她 在 厨 房 里 做 饭 。
tā zài chú fáng lǐ zuò fàn

She is cooking **in** the kitchen

214 里边　　　lǐ bian　　　**Noun: inside**

我 的 书 在 柜 子 里 边 。
wǒ de shū zài guì zi lǐ bian

My book is **inside** the cabinet.

215 两　　　liǎng　　　**Number: two**

我 早 上 吃 了 两 个 橘 子 。
wǒ zǎo shàng chī le liǎng gè jú zi

I ate **two** oranges in the morning.

216 零　　　líng　　　**Number: zero**

二 零 二 零 年 发 生 了 新 冠 疫 情 。
èr líng èr líng nián fā shēng le xīn guàn yì qíng

In 2020, the coronavirus pandemic happened.

217 六   liù   **Number: six**

wǒ de gōng sī yǒu liù gè bù mén
我 的 公 司 有 六 个 部 门 。
My company has **six** departments.

218 楼   lóu   **Noun: floor; building**

wǒ de péng yǒu zhù zài èr lóu
我 的 朋 友 住 在 二 楼 。
My friend lives on the second **floor**.

zhè shì gōng sī de bàn gōng lóu
这 是 公 司 的 办 公 楼 。
This is the company's office **building**.

219 楼上   lóu shàng   **Noun: upstairs**

wǒ de lín jū zhù zài lóu shàng
我 的 邻 居 住 在 楼 上 。
My neighbour lives **upstairs**.

220 楼下   lóu xià   **Noun: downstairs**

lóu xià yǒu gè shāng diàn
楼 下 有 个 商 店 。
There is a shop **downstairs**.

221 路   lù   **Noun: road**

zhè tiáo lù zài shī gōng
这 条 路 在 施 工 。
This **road** is under construction.

222 路口　lù kǒu　Noun: intersection

duì bù qǐ, lù kǒu bù néng tíng chē
对 不 起 , 路 口 不 能 停 车 。

Sorry, you cannot park at the **intersection**.

223 路上　lù shàng　Noun: on the road

wǒ cháng cháng zài zhè tiáo lù shàng qí chē
我 常 常 在 这 条 路 上 骑 车 。

I often cycle **on this road**.

224 妈妈　mā ma　Noun: mother

wǒ mā ma shì kuài jì
我 妈 妈 是 会 计 。

My **mother** is an accountant.

225 马路　mǎ lù　Noun: pedestrian crossing

lǜ dēng liàng le, wǒ men guò mǎ lù ba
绿 灯 亮 了 , 我 们 过 马 路 吧 。

The green light is on, let's cross the **road** (**pedestrian crossing**).

226 马上　mǎ shàng　Adverb: immediately

bié dān xīn, wǒ mǎ shàng kāi chē qù nǐ jiā
别 担 心 , 我 马 上 开 车 去 你 家 。

Don't worry, I will drive to your home **immediately**.

227 吗　ma　indicate a question

nǐ kě yǐ bāng wǒ ma
你 可 以 帮 我 吗 ?

Can you help me?

228 买　　　　　mǎi　　　　　**Verb: to buy**

wǒ yào qù chāo shì mǎi yī píng hóng jiǔ
我 要 去 超 市 买 一 瓶 红 酒 。
I am going to the supermarket **to buy** a bottle of red wine.

229 慢　　　　　màn　　　　　**Adjective: slow**

zài xīng qī yī, shí jiān guò dé hěn màn
在 星 期 一 , 时 间 过 得 很 慢 。
On Mondays, time passes very **slow**.

230 忙　　　　　máng　　　　　**Adjective: busy**

wǒ zhè gè yuè tài máng le
我 这 个 月 太 忙 了 。
I am too **busy** this month.

231 毛　　　　　máo　　　　　**Noun: fur; hair**

zhè tiáo gǒu de máo hěn bái
这 条 狗 的 毛 很 白 !
This dog's **fur** is very white!

232 没　　　　　méi　　　　　**Verb: not**

wǒ méi qù guò fǎ guó
我 没 去 过 法 国 。
I have **not** been to France.

233 没关系　　　méi guān xi　　　**Phrase: never mind; it's okay**

méi guān xi, nǐ bù yòng dào qiàn
没 关 系 , 你 不 用 道 歉 。
It's okay, you don't need to apologize.

234 没什么　méi shén me　**Phrase: It's nothing**

méi shén me　gāi dān xīn de
没什么 该 担 心 的 。
There is nothing to worry about.

235 没事儿　méi shì er　**Phrase: It's fine**

bié dān xīn，méi shì er
别 担 心 ， 没 事 儿 。
Don't worry, **it's fine**.

236 没有　méi yǒu　**Verb: not have**

tā yǒu dì di，méi yǒu gē ge
他 有 弟 弟 ， 没 有 哥 哥 。
He has a younger brother, but **doesn't have** an older brother.

237 妹妹　mèi mei　**Noun: younger sister**

wǒ mèi mei shì dà xué shēng
我 妹 妹 是 大 学 生 。
My **younger sister** is a university student.

238 门　mén　**Noun: door**

wǒ jiā fáng zi yǒu qián mén，yě yǒu hòu mén
我 家 房 子 有 前 门 ， 也 有 后 门 。
My house has a front **door** and a back **door**.

239 门口　mén kǒu　**Noun: door way**

tā zài mén kǒu chōu yān
他 在 门 口 抽 烟 。
He is smoking at the **door way**.

240 门票   mén piào   **Noun: entrance ticket**

wǒ yào mǎi liǎng zhāng mén piào
我 要 买 两 张 门 票 。
I want to buy two **tickets**.

241 们   men   **indicate plural (personal pronouns)**

wǒ men yào qù zhōng guó lǚ yóu
我 们 要 去 中 国 旅 游 。
We are going to travel to China.

242 米饭   mǐ fàn   **Noun: cooked rice**

fú wù yuán qǐng gěi wǒ yī wǎn mǐ fàn
服 务 员 ，请 给 我 一 碗 米 饭 。
Waitetress, please give me a bowl of **rice**.

243 面包   miàn bāo   **Noun: bread**

wǒ chī le jǐ kuài miàn bāo
我 吃 了 几 块 面 包 。
I ate a few pieces of **bread**.

244 面条   miàn tiáo   **Noun: noodle**

wǒ hěn xǐ huān chī yì dà lì miàn tiáo
我 很 喜 欢 吃 意 大 利 面 条 。
I like eating Italian **noodles**.

245 名字   míng zì   **Noun: name**

wǒ de zhōng wén míng zì shì dà wéi
我 的 中 文 名 字 是 大 为 。
My Chinese name is Dawei!

246 明白   míng bái   **Verb: to understand**

_{duì bù qǐ wǒ bù míng bái nǐ de huà}
对 不 起 , 我 不 明 白 你 的 话 。
Sorry, I don't **understand** what you said.

247 明年   míng nián   **Noun: next year**

_{wǒ míng nián yào qù dé guó liú xué}
我 明 年 要 去 德 国 留 学 。
I am going to study in Germany **next year**.

248 明天   míng tiān   **Noun: tomorrow**

_{wǒ míng tiān yào qù cān jiā hūn lǐ}
我 明 天 要 去 参 加 婚 礼 。
I am going to attend a wedding **tomorrow**.

249 拿   ná   **Verb: to hold; take**

_{nǐ kě yǐ bāng wǒ ná yī xià bāo ma}
你 可 以 帮 我 拿 一 下 包 吗 ?
Could you help me to **hold** my bag?

250 哪   nǎ   **Pronoun: which**

_{nǐ shì nǎ guó rén}
你 是 哪 国 人 ?
Which country are you from?

251 哪里   nǎ lǐ   **Pronoun: where**

_{nǐ zhī dào jiǔ diàn zài nǎ lǐ ma}
你 知 道 酒 店 在 哪 里 吗 ?
Do you know **where** the hotel is?

252 哪儿　　　nǎ'er　　　**Pronoun: where**

nǐ zhù zài nǎ ér
你 住 在 哪 儿 ？
Where do you live?

253 哪些　　　nǎ xiē　　　**Pronoun: which ones**

qǐng wèn nǎ xiē shì nǐ de wén jiàn
请 问 , 哪 些 是 你 的 文 件 ？
Excuse me, **which ones** are your files?

254 那　　　nà　　　**Pronoun: that**

nà shì wǒ men bù mén de jīng lǐ
那 是 我 们 部 门 的 经 理 。
That is the manager of our department.

255 那边　　　nà biān　　　**Noun: over there**

wǒ men kě yǐ zài nà biān tíng chē
我 们 可 以 在 那 边 停 车 。
We can park the car **over there**.

256 那里　　　nà lǐ　　　**Pronoun: that place**

wǒ xiǎng qù nà lǐ sàn bù
我 想 去 那 里 散 步 。
I want to go to **that place** for a walk.

257 那儿　　　nà'er　　　**Pronoun: there**

wǒ měi tiān dōu qù nà er liù gǒu
我 每 天 都 去 那 儿 遛 狗 。
I go **there** every day to walk dogs.

59

258 那些　　　　nà xiē　　　**Pronoun: those**

nà xiē shì nǐ de tóng shì ma
那 些 是 你 的 同 事 吗 ?

Are **those** your colleagues?

259 奶　　　　nǎi　　　**Noun: milk**

wǒ měi tiān zǎo shàng dōu hē niú nǎi
我 每 天 早 上 都 喝 牛 奶 。

I drink (cow) **milk** every morning.

260 奶奶　　　　nǎi nai　　　**Noun: paternal-grandma**

wǒ de nǎi nai jīn nián jiǔ shí suì le
我 的 奶 奶 今 年 九 十 岁 了 。

My **grandma** is ninety years old this year.

261 男　　　　nán　　　**Noun: male; man**

qǐng wèn nán cè suǒ zài nǎ
请 问 , 男 厕 所 在 哪 ?

Excuse me, where is the **men's** toilet?

262 男孩　　　　nán hái　　　**Noun: boy**

zhè gè nán hái duō dà le
这 个 男 孩 多 大 了 ?

How old is this **boy**?

263 男朋友　　　　nán péng yǒu　　　**Noun: boyfriend**

wǒ hé wǒ de nán péng yǒu jiāo wǎng sān nián le
我 和 我 的 男 朋 友 交 往 三 年 了 。

My **boyfriend** and I have been dating for three years.

264 男人   nán rén   **Noun: man (adult)**

xiǎo tōu shì gè zhōng nián nán rén
小 偷 是 个 中 年 男 人 。
The thief is a middle-aged **man**.

265 男生   nán shēng   **Noun: young man; guy**

zhè xiē nán shēng zài zhè lǐ shàng dà xué
这 些 男 生 在 这 里 上 大 学 。
These **guys** are attending university here.

266 南   nán   **Noun: south; southern**

wǒ de fáng zi xiàng nán
我 的 房 子 向 南 。
My house faces **south** .

267 南边   nán bian   **Noun: south side**

huā yuán zài fáng zi de nán bian
花 园 在 房 子 的 南 边 。
The garden is on the **south side** of the house.

268 难   nán   **Adjective: difficult**

wǒ jué dé xué zhōng wén bù nán
我 觉 得 学 中 文 不 难 。
I think learning Chinese is not **difficult**.

269 呢   ne   **indicate question "what about"**

wǒ shì fǎ guó rén nǐ ne
我 是 法 国 人 , 你 呢 ？
I am French, **what about** you?

270 能　　　　néng　　　　**Verb: can; able to**

duì bù qǐ，wǒ míng tiān bù néng hé nǐ qù kàn diàn yǐng
对 不 起 , 我 明 天 不 能 和 你 去 看 电 影 。
Sorry, I **can**not go to see the movie with you tomorrow.

271 你　　　　nǐ　　　　**Noun: you (singular)**

qǐng wèn，nǐ zài nǎ gè bù mén gōng zuò
请 问 , 你 在 哪 个 部 门 工 作 ?
May I ask, which department do **you** work in?

272 你们　　　　nǐ men　　　　**Noun: you (plural)**

nǐ men xiǎng qù jiǔ ba ma
你 们 想 去 酒 吧 吗 ?
Do **you** (plural) want to go to the pub?

273 年　　　　nián　　　　**Noun: year**

tā men jié hūn shí nián le
他 们 结 婚 十 年 了 。
They have been married for ten **years**.

274 您　　　　nín　　　　**Noun: you (courteous)**

qǐng wèn，nín xū yào bāng zhù ma
请 问 , 您 需 要 帮 助 吗 ?
Excuse me, do **you** need help?

275 牛奶　　　　niú nǎi　　　　**Noun: milk (cow)**

wǒ měi tiān zǎo shàng hē yī bēi niú nǎi
我 每 天 早 上 喝 一 杯 牛 奶 。
I drink a glass of **milk** every morning.

276 女   nǚ   **Adjective: female; woman**

qǐng wèn, nǚ cè suǒ zài nǎ ér?
请 问，女 厕 所 在 哪 儿 ？
Excuse me, where is the **women**'s toilet?

277 女儿   nǚ'ér   **Noun: daughter**

wáng xiān shēng yǒu liǎng gè nǚ ér。
王 先 生 有 两 个 女 儿 。
Mr. Wang has two **daughters**.

278 女孩   nǚ hái   **Noun: girl**

zhè gè nǚ hái zài nǎ lǐ shàng xué?
这 个 女 孩 在 哪 里 上 学 ？
Where does this **girl** go to school?

279 女朋友   nǚ péng yǒu   **Noun: girlfriend**

tā shàng gè yuè hé nǚ péng yǒu fēn shǒu le。
他 上 个 月 和 女 朋 友 分 手 了 。
He broke up with his **girlfriend** last month.

280 女人   nǚ rén   **Noun: woman**

zài wǒ men gōng sī, nǚ rén bǐ nán rén duō。
在 我 们 公 司 ，女 人 比 男 人 多 。
In our company, there are more **women** than men.

281 女生   nǚ shēng   **Noun: young woman; girl**

nà gè nǚ shēng shì wǒ de dà xué tóng xué。
那 个 女 生 是 我 的 大 学 同 学 。
That **young woman** is my university classmate.

282 旁边

páng biān

Noun: next to; nearby

gōng yuán páng biān shì yī tiáo hé
公园 旁边 是 一 条 河。

There is a river **next to** the park.

283 跑

pǎo

Verb: run

zhè tiáo gǒu pǎo dé hěn kuài
这 条 狗 跑 得 很 快。

This **dog** runs very fast.

284 朋友

péng yǒu

Noun: friend

tā shì wǒ zuì hǎo de péng yǒu
他 是 我 最 好 的 朋 友。

He is my best **friend**.

285 票

piào

Noun: ticket

wǒ yào mǎi liǎng zhāng dì tiě piào
我 要 买 两 张 地 铁 票。

I want to buy two subway **tickets**.

286 七

qī

Number: seven

wǒ de nǚ ér jīn nián qī suì
我 的 女 儿 今 年 七 岁。

My daughter is **seven** years old this year.

287 起

qǐ

Verb: start

cóng jīn tiān qǐ tā shì wǒ men de xīn zhǔ guǎn
从 今 天 起，他 是 我 们 的 新 主 管。

Starting from today, he is our new director.

288 起床　qǐ chuáng　**Verb: to get up (from bed)**

tā měi tiān zǎo shàng liù diǎn bàn qǐ chuáng
她 每 天 早 上 六 点 半 起 床 。
She **gets up** at half past six every morning.

289 起来　qǐ lái　**Verb: to rise up**

rán hòu tā cóng dì shàng zhàn qǐ lái
然 后 , 他 从 地 上 站 起 来 。
Then, he stood **up** from the ground.

290 汽车　qì chē　**Noun: automobile (e.g. car, bus)**

wǒ bà ba mǎi le yī liàng qì chē
我 爸 爸 买 了 一 辆 汽 车 。
My dad bought a **car**.

291 前　qián　**Noun: front; ago**

nǐ xiàng qián zǒu yī bǎi mǐ jiù dào
你 向 前 走 一 百 米 , 就 到 。
Walk forwards (towards **front**) for 100 meters, then you will arrive.

yī nián qián tā kāi shǐ xué xí zhōng wén
一 年 前 , 他 开 始 学 习 中 文 。
A year **ago**, he started learning Chinese.

292 前边　qián bian　**Noun: in front**

qián bian yǒu gè jiǔ ba
前 边 有 个 酒 吧 。
There is a pub **in front**.

65

293 前天　　qián tiān　　**Noun: the day before yesterday**

<small>wǒ qián tiān zuò huǒ chē qù le lún dūn</small>
我 前 天 坐 火 车 去 了 伦 敦 。

I took the train to London **the day before yesterday**.

294 钱　　qián　　**Noun: money**

<small>qǐng wèn zhè píng pí jiǔ duō shǎo qián</small>
请 问 , 这 瓶 啤 酒 多 少 钱 ？

Excuse me, how much **(money)** is this bottle of beer?

295 钱包　　qián bāo　　**Noun: wallet**

<small>wǒ yào mǎi gè qián bāo sòng gěi tā</small>
我 要 买 个 钱 包 送 给 他 。

I want to buy a **wallet** for him.

296 请　　qǐng　　**Verb: to invite**

<small>tā qǐng wǒ men cān jiā tā de shēng rì jù huì</small>
他 请 我 们 参 加 他 的 生 日 聚 会 。

He **invited** us to join his birthday party.

297 请假　　qǐng jià　　**Verb: ask for leave**

<small>nǐ yīng gāi dǎ diàn huà gěi jīng lǐ qǐng jià</small>
你 应 该 打 电 话 给 经 理 请 假 。

You should call the manager to **ask for leave**.

298 请进　　qǐng jìn　　**Phrase: please come in**

<small>huān yíng nǐ men qǐng jìn</small>
欢 迎 你 们 , 请 进 。

Welcome, **please come in**.

299 请问　　qǐng wèn　　**Verb: excuse me; may I ask**

qǐng wèn，nǐ zài nǎ lǐ gōng zuò？
请 问 ，你 在 哪 里 工 作 ？
May I ask, where do you work?

---

300 请坐　　qǐng zuò　　**Phrase: please sit down**

yǐ zi zài zhè ér，qǐng zuò。
椅 子 在 这 儿 ，请 坐 。
The chair is here, **please sit down**.

---

301 球　　qiú　　**Noun: ball**

wǒ men xià wǔ qù tī zú qiú，hǎo ma？
我 们 下 午 去 踢 足 球 ，好 吗 ？
Let's go to play foot**ball** in the afternoon, OK?

---

302 去　　qù　　**Verb: to go to**

míng nián chūn tiān，wǒ yào qù pá cháng chéng。
明 年 春 天 ，我 要 去 爬 长 城 。
Next spring, I am **going to** climb the Great Wall.

---

303 去年　　qù nián　　**Noun: last year**

wǒ men shì qù nián rèn shí de。
我 们 是 去 年 认 识 的 。
We met **last year**.

---

304 热　　rè　　**Adjective: hot**

jīn nián xià tiān，tiān qì fēi cháng rè。
今 年 夏 天 ，天 气 非 常 热 。
This summer, the weather is very **hot**.

305 人   rén   **Noun: people; person**

wǒ men gōng sī yī gòng yǒu wǔ shí gè rén
我 们 公 司 一 共 有 五 十 个 人 。
Our company has 50 **people** in total.

306 认识   rèn shí   **Verb: to know (somebody)**

nǐ men shì zěn me rèn shí de
你 们 是 怎 么 认 识 的 ？
How do you **know** each other?

307 认真   rèn zhēn   **Adjective: serious**

tā duì nǚ péng yǒu bù tài rèn zhēn
他 对 女 朋 友 不 太 认 真 。
He is not too **serious** about his girlfriend.

308 日   rì   **Noun: day**

shèng dàn jié shì shí èr yuè èr shí wǔ rì
圣 诞 节 是 十 二 月 二 十 五 日 。
Chrismas is on the 25th **day** of December.

309 日期   rì qi   **Noun: date**

wǒ bù jì dé tā men de jié hūn rì qi
我 不 记 得 他 们 的 结 婚 日 期 。
I don't remember their wedding **date**.

310 肉   ròu   **Noun: meat**

tā shì sù shí zhǔ yì zhě bù chī ròu
他 是 素 食 主 义 者 ， 不 吃 肉 。
He is a vegetarian and does not eat **meat**.

311 三   sān   **Number: three**

wǒ jīn tiān zǎo shàng chī le sān gè bāo zi
我 今 天 早 上 吃 了 三 个 包 子 。
I ate **three** steamed buns this morning.

312 山   shān   **Noun: mountain**

wǒ men zhōu mò qù pá shān hǎo ma
我 们 周 末 去 爬 山 , 好 吗 ?
Let's go to climb the **mountain** on the weekend, OK?

313 商场   shāng chǎng   **Noun: shopping mall**

shì zhōng xīn yǒu yī gè dà shāng chǎng
市 中 心 有 一 个 大 商 场 。
There is a big **shopping mall** in the city centre.

314 商店   shāng diàn   **Noun: shop**

tā qù shāng diàn mǎi bīng qí lín le
他 去 商 店 买 冰 淇 淋 了 。
He went to the **shop** to buy ice cream.

315 上   shàng   **Preposition: on Verb: to ascend**

Prep.

zhuō zi shàng yǒu liǎng tái diàn nǎo
桌 子 上 有 两 台 电 脑 。
There are two computers **on** the desk.

Verb

nǐ kě yǐ zuò diàn tī shàng lóu
你 可 以 坐 电 梯 上 楼 。
You can take the elevator to **go upstairs**.

316 上班 shàng bān **Verb: to work**

tā zài yín háng shàng bān
她 在 银 行 上 班 。
She **works** in the bank.

317 上边 shàng bian **Noun: top of; upside**

shù zhī shàng bian yǒu yī zhī hóu zi
树 枝 上 边 有 一 只 猴 子 。
There is a monkey on the **top of** the branch.

318 上车 shàng chē **Verb: get in (vehicle)**

sī jī qǐng wǒ men shàng chē
司 机 请 我 们 上 车 。
The driver asked us to **get in the car**.

319 上次 shàng cì **Phrase: last time**

wǒ shàng cì qù zhōng guó shì zài chūn tiān
我 上 次 去 中 国 是 在 春 天 。
Last time I went to China was in spring.

320 上课 shàng kè **Verb: have class**

wǒ měi xīng qī liù zǎo shàng shí diǎn shàng kè
我 每 星 期 六 早 上 十 点 上 课 。
I **have class** at ten o'clock every Saturday morning.

321 上网 shàng wǎng **Verb: go online**

tā cháng cháng shàng wǎng dǎ yóu xì
他 常 常 上 网 打 游 戏 。
He often **goes online** to play games.

322 上午   shàng wǔ   **Noun: morning**

wǒ jīn tiān shàng wǔ zài jiā shàng bān
我 今 天 上 午 在 家 上 班 。
I worked at home this **morning**.

323 上学   shàng xué   **Verb: go to school**

wǒ dì di bù xǐ huān shàng xué
我 弟 弟 不 喜 欢 上 学 。
My brother doesn't like **going to school**.

324a 少   shǎo   **Adjective: few; little**

wǒ zuì jìn chī dé hěn shǎo
我 最 近 吃 得 很 少 。
I have eaten very **little** recently.

324b 少   shào   **Adjective: young**

zhè qún shào nián zài tī zú qiú
这 群 少 年 在 踢 足 球 。
This group of **young**sters are playing football.

325 谁   shéi   **Pronoun: who**

nǐ zhī dào tā shì shéi ma
你 知 道 她 是 谁 吗 ？
Do you know **who** she is?

326 身上   shēn shàng   **Noun: on one's body**

tā shēn shàng chuān zhe yī jiàn bái chèn shān
他 身 上 穿 着 一 件 白 衬 衫 。
He is wearing a white shirt **on his body**.

327 身体 shēn tǐ **Noun: body; health**

wǒ fù mǔ de shēn tǐ hěn hǎo
我 父 母 的 身 体 很 好 。
My parents are in good **health**.

328 什么 shén me **Pronoun: what**

nǐ zuì xǐ huān shén me yán sè
你 最 喜 欢 什 么 颜 色 ?
What color do you like the most?

329 生病 shēng bìng **Verb: get sick**

tā shēng bìng le xiàn zài zài yī yuàn
他 生 病 了 ， 现 在 在 医 院 。
He **got sick** and now in the hospital.

330 生气 shēng qì **Adjective: angry**

tā hěn shēng qì bù xiǎng gēn wǒ shuō huà
他 很 生 气 ， 不 想 跟 我 说 话 。
He is very **angry** and doesn't want to talk to me.

331 生日 shēng rì **Noun: birthday**

wǒ men míng tiān qù cān jiā tā de shēng rì jù huì
我 们 明 天 去 参 加 他 的 生 日 聚 会 。
We will go to attend his **birthday** party tomorrow.

332 十 shí **Number: ten**

jīn tiān nǐ shí suì zhù nǐ shēng rì kuài lè
今 天 你 十 岁 ， 祝 你 生 日 快 乐 !
Today you are **ten** years old, happy birthday to you!

333 时候   shí hòu   **Noun: a point in (time)**

zài zhōng guó de shí hòu wǒ cháng cháng chī jiǎo zi
在 中 国 的 时 候 ，我 常 常 吃 饺 子 。
During my **time** in China, I often ate dumplings.

334 时间   shí jiān   **Noun: time**

xiàn zài shì shàng bān shí jiān tā hěn máng
现 在 是 上 班 时 间 ，他 很 忙 。
It's working **time** now, he is very busy.

335 事   shì   **Noun: matter**

qǐng wèn nǐ yǒu shén me shì
请 问 ，你 有 什 么 事 ？
Excuse me, what's the **matter** (you have)?

336 试   shì   **Verb: to try**

wǒ kě yǐ shì chuān zhè jiàn yī fú ma
我 可 以 试 穿 这 件 衣 服 吗 ？
May I **try** on this item of clothing?

337 是   shì   **Verb: to be**

zhè shì wǒ de nǚ péng yǒu jiào xiǎo yún
这 是 我 的 女 朋 友 ，叫 小 云 。
This **is** my girlfriend, called Xiaoyun.

338 是不是   shì bù shì   **Phrase: yes or no**

nǐ xiǎng gēn tā jié hūn shì bù shì
你 想 跟 她 结 婚 ，是 不 是 ？
You want to marry her, **yes or no**?

73

339 手   shǒu   **Noun: hands**

nǐ děng yī děng, wǒ qù xǐ shǒu
你 等 一 等 , 我 去 洗 手 。

Please wait a bit, I am going to wash **hands**.

340 手机   shǒu jī   **Noun: phone**

zhè shì wǒ gāng mǎi de píng guǒ shǒu jī
这 是 我 刚 买 的 苹 果 手 机 。

This is the iPhone (apple **phone**) I just bought.

341 书   shū   **Noun: book**

tā de shū jià shàng yǒu hěn duō shū
他 的 书 架 上 有 很 多 书 。

There are many **books** on his bookshelf.

342 书包   shū bāo   **Noun: schoolbag**

wǒ yào gěi nǚ ér mǎi yī gè xīn shū bāo
我 要 给 女 儿 买 一 个 新 书 包 。

I want to buy a new **schoolbag** for my daughter.

343 书店   shū diàn   **Noun: bookstore**

shì zhōng xīn yǒu jǐ gè shū diàn
市 中 心 有 几 个 书 店 。

There are several **bookstores** in the city centre.

344 树   shù   **Noun: tree**

tīng shuō, zhè kē dà shù yǒu wǔ bǎi suì le
听 说 , 这 颗 大 树 有 五 百 岁 了 。

I heard this big **tree** is 500 years old.

345 水   shuǐ   **Noun: water**

nǐ kě yǐ bāng wǒ dào yī bēi shuǐ ma
你 可 以 帮 我 倒 一 杯 水 吗？
Can you pour me a glass of **water**?

346 水果   shuǐ guǒ   **Noun: fruits**

wǒ jiā chú fáng yǒu hěn duō shuǐ guǒ
我 家 厨 房 有 很 多 水 果 。
There are many **fruits** in my kitchen.

347 睡   shuì   **Verb: to sleep**

wǒ zuó tiān wǎn shàng shuì dé bù tài hǎo
我 昨 天 晚 上 睡 得 不 太 好 。
I didn't **sleep** well last night.

348 睡觉   shuì jiào   **Verb: go to sleep**

wǒ měi tiān wǎn shàng shí yī diǎn shuì jiào
我 每 天 晚 上 十 一 点 睡 觉 。
I **go to sleep** at eleven every night.

349 说   shuō   **Verb: speak**

wǒ huì shuō zhōng wén hé yīng wén
我 会 说 中 文 和 英 文 。
I can **speak** Chinese and English.

350 说话   shuō huà   **Verb: to talk**

gēn tā shuō huà wǒ jué dé hěn kāi xīn
跟 她 说 话 ，我 觉 得 很 开 心 。
Talking with her, I feel very happy.

351 四　　　sì　　　**Number: four**

wǒ de zhí zi jīn nián sì suì le
我 的 侄 子 今 年 四 岁 了 。
My nephew is **four** years old this year.

352 送　　　sòng　　　**Verb: to accompany; to deliver**

wǒ huì kāi chē sòng tā huí jiā
我 会 开 车 送 她 回 家 。
I will drive to **accompany** her home.

kuài dì yuán lái sòng bāo guǒ le
快 递 员 来 送 包 裹 了 。
The postman is here to **deliver** the parcel.

353 岁　　　suì　　　**Noun: age**

wǒ de zhí nǚ xià gè yuè jiù bā suì le
我 的 侄 女 下 个 月 就 八 岁 了 。
My niece will be **eight years old** next month.

354 他　　　tā　　　**Pronoun: him; he**

tā shì wǒ men bù mén de zhǔ guǎn
他 是 我 们 部 门 的 主 管 。
He is the head of our department.

355 他们　　　tā men　　　**Pronoun: them; they**

tā men dōu shì wǒ de tóng shì
他 们 都 是 我 的 同 事 。
They are all my colleagues.

356 她　　　tā　　　Pronoun: she; her

tā shì wǒ de mì shū
她 是 我 的 秘 书 。

She is my secretary.

357 她们　　　tā men　　　Pronoun: they; them (female)

tā men dōu shì hěn bàng de yùn dòng yuán
她 们 都 是 很 棒 的 运 动 员 。

They are all great athletes.

358 太　　　tài　　　Adverb: very; too

tā zuò de cài tài hǎo chī le
她 做 的 菜 太 好 吃 了 。

The dishes she cooks are **too** delicious!

359 天　　　tiān　　　Noun: day

wǒ men dǎ suàn qù jiā zhōu dù jià wǔ tiān
我 们 打 算 去 加 州 度 假 五 天 。

We plan to go to California for a five-**day** holiday.

360 天气　　　tiān qì　　　Noun: weather

jīn nián xià tiān de tiān qì fēi cháng hǎo
今 年 夏 天 的 天 气 非 常 好 ！

The **weather** this summer is very good!

361 听　　　tīng　　　Verb: listen

nǐ tīng hǎo xiàng yǒu hái zi zài kū
你 听 ， 好 像 有 孩 子 在 哭 。

Listen, it sounds like a child is crying.

77

362 听到　tīng dào　**Verb: to have heard**

wǒ tīng dào le tā men de qiāo qiāo huà
我 听 到 了 他 们 的 悄 悄 话 。

I've **heard** their whispers.

363 听见　tīng jiàn　**Verb: to hear**

kāi shǐ xià yǔ le nǐ tīng jiàn le ma
开 始 下 雨 了 , 你 听 见 了 吗 ?

It has started raining, can you **hear** it?

364 听写　tīng xiě　**Verb: to dictate**

wǒ men xiàn zài kāi shǐ tīng xiě shēng cí
我 们 现 在 开 始 听 写 生 词 。

Let's start **dictating** new vocabularies now.

365 同学　tóng xué　**Noun: classmate**

wǒ men bān yǒu èr shí gè tóng xué
我 们 班 有 二 十 个 同 学 。

There are twenty **classmates** in our class.

366 图书馆　tú shū guǎn　**Noun: library**

wǒ men dà xué yǒu yī gè hěn dà de tú shū guǎn
我 们 大 学 有 一 个 很 大 的 图 书 馆 。

Our university has a very big **library**.

367 外　wài　**Noun: exterior**

mén wài zhàn zhe yī gè sòng huò yuán
门 外 站 着 一 个 送 货 员 。

A delivery man is standing by the door (**exterior**).

368 外边   wài bian   **Noun: outside**

tā zài wài bian hé xiǎo gǒu wán
她 在 外 边 和 小 狗 玩 。
She is playing with the puppy **outside**.

369 外国   wài guó   **Noun: foreign (country)**

wǒ yǒu hěn duō wài guó péng yǒu
我 有 很 多 外 国 朋 友 。
I have many **foreign** friends.

370 外语   wài yǔ   **Noun: foreign language**

zhōng wén shì hěn yǒu qù de wài yǔ
中 文 是 很 有 趣 的 外 语 。
Chinese is a very interesting **foreign language**.

371 玩（儿）   wán er   **Verb: to play; have fun**

hái zi men zài gōng yuán lǐ wán er
孩 子 们 在 公 园 里 玩 儿 。
The children are **playing** in the park.

372 晚   wǎn   **Adjective: late**

tā jīn tiān xià bān dé hěn wǎn
他 今 天 下 班 得 很 晚 。
He got off work **late** today.

373 晚饭   wǎn fàn   **Noun: dinner**

wǒ men míng tiān qù péng yǒu jiā chī wǎn fàn
我 们 明 天 去 朋 友 家 吃 晚 饭 。
We will go to a friend's house for **dinner** tomorrow.

374 晚上   wǎn shàng   **Noun: night**

wǒ měi tiān wǎn shàng dōu huì kàn xiǎo shuō
我 每 天 晚 上 都 会 看 小 说 。
I read novels every **night**.

375 网上   wǎng shàng   **Noun: online**

wǒ men jīng cháng zài wǎng shàng mǎi dōng xī
我 们 经 常 在 网 上 买 东 西 。
We often buy things **online**.

376 网友   wǎng yǒu   **Noun: online friend**

wǒ de wēi xìn shàng yǒu hěn duō wǎng yǒu
我 的 微 信 上 有 很 多 网 友 。
I have many **online friends** on my WeChat.

377 忘   wàng   **Verb: to forget**

wǒ tài máng le wàng le hē kā fēi
我 太 忙 了 , 忘 了 喝 咖 啡 。
I was so busy that I **forgot** to drink coffee.

379 问   wèn   **Verb: to ask**

wǒ kě yǐ wèn nǐ yī gè wèn tí ma
我 可 以 问 你 一 个 问 题 吗 ?
May I **ask** you a question?

380 我   wǒ   **Pronoun: I; me**

wǒ xiǎng dāng yī míng lǜ shī
我 想 当 一 名 律 师 。
I want to be a lawyer.

381 我们　wǒ men　**Pronoun: we; us**

wǒ men qù gōng yuán sàn bù hǎo ma
我 们 去 公 园 散 步 , 好 吗 ?
Shall **we** go to walk in the park?

382 五　wǔ　**Number: five**

wǒ jiā de mǔ gǒu shēng le wǔ zhǐ xiǎo gǒu
我 家 的 母 狗 生 了 五 只 小 狗 。
My family's female dog gave birth to **five** puppies.

383 午饭　wǔ fàn　**Noun: lunch meal**

wǒ yī bān shí èr diǎn chī wǔ fàn
我 一 般 十 二 点 吃 午 饭 。
I usually have **lunch (meal)** at twelve.

384 西　xī　**Noun: west**

wǎng xī zǒu wǔ fēn zhōng jiù dào
往 西 走 五 分 钟 就 到 。
Walk **west** for 5 minutes, then you will arrive.

385 西边　xī biān　**Noun: west side**

xī zàng zài zhōng guó de xī biān
西 藏 在 中 国 的 西 边 。
Tibet is on the **west side** of China.

386 洗　xǐ　**Verb: to wash**

wǒ yǒu xǐ wǎn jī bù yòng zì jǐ xǐ wǎn
我 有 洗 碗 机 , 不 用 自 己 洗 碗 。
I have a dishwasher, no need to **wash** dishes myself.

387 洗手间　　xǐ shǒu jiān　　**Noun: toilet**

请 问 ，洗 手 间 在 哪 儿 ？
qǐng wèn xǐ shǒu jiān zài nǎ ér

Excuse me, where is the **toilet**?

388 喜欢　　xǐ huān　　**Verb: to like**

我 喜 欢 开 车 去 郊 区 玩 。
wǒ xǐ huān kāi chē qù jiāo qū wán

I **like** to drive to the suburbs to hang out.

389 下　　xià　　**Noun: down; under**

树 下 有 一 把 椅 子 。
shù xià yǒu yī bǎ yǐ zi

There is a chair **under** the tree.

390 下班　　xià bān　　**Verb: finish work**

我 每 天 下 午 五 点 半 下 班 。
wǒ měi tiān xià wǔ wǔ diǎn bàn xià bān

I **finish work** at half past five every afternoon.

391 下边　　xià bian　　**Noun: underneath**

桌 子 下 边 有 两 条 狗 。
zhuō zi xià bian yǒu liǎng tiáo gǒu

There are two dogs **underneath** the table.

392 下车　　xià chē　　**Verb: to get off (vehicle)**

我 要 在 飞 机 场 下 车 。
wǒ yào zài fēi jī chǎng xià chē

I want to **get off** at the airport.

393 下次　　　xià cì　　　**Noun: next time**

wǒ men xià cì zài nǎ lǐ jiàn miàn
我 们 下 次 在 哪 里 见 面 ？
Where shall we meet **next time**?

394 下课　　　xià kè　　　**Verb: finish class**

wǒ shí diǎn bàn xià kè nǐ ne
我 十 点 半 下 课 ， 你 呢 ？
I **finish class** at half past ten, how about you?

395 下午　　　xià wǔ　　　**Noun: afternoon**

wǒ jīn tiān xià wǔ yǒu sān gè huì yì
我 今 天 下 午 有 三 个 会 议 。
I have three meetings this **afternoon**.

396 下雨　　　xià yǔ　　　**Verb: to rain**

tiān qì yù bào shuō wǎn shàng huì xià yǔ
天 气 预 报 说 晚 上 会 下 雨 。
The weather forecast says it will **rain** at night.

397 先　　　xiān　　　**Adverb: first**

wǒ yào xiān chī fàn rán hòu kàn zú qiú sài
我 要 先 吃 饭 ， 然 后 看 足 球 赛 。
I want to eat **first**, then watch the football match.

398 先生　　xiān sheng　　Noun: Mr. gentleman

zhāng xiān sheng hěn gāo xìng rèn shí nǐ
张 先 生 , 很 高 兴 认 识 你 。
Mr. Zhang, nice to meet you.

nǚ shì men xiān sheng men wǎn huì xiàn zài kāi shǐ
女 士 们 , 先 生 们 ! 晚 会 现 在 开 始 。
Ladies, **gentlemen**, the party starts now.

399 现在　　xiàn zài　　Noun: now

xiàn zài jǐ diǎn le
现 在 几 点 了 ?
What time is it **now**?

400 想　　xiǎng　　Verb: to think; want

zhè gè xīng qī wǔ wǒ bù xiǎng shàng bān
这 个 星 期 五 , 我 不 想 上 班 。
This Friday, I don't **want** to go to work.

401 小　　xiǎo　　Adjective: small

zhè jiàn yī fú tài xiǎo wǒ bù néng chuān
这 件 衣 服 太 小 , 我 不 能 穿 。
This item of clothing is too **small**, I cannot wear it.

402 小孩(儿)　　xiǎo hái er　　Noun: kid; chid

zhè gè xiǎo hái shì wǒ de zhí zi
这 个 小 孩 是 我 的 侄 子 。
This **kid** is my nephew.

403 小姐　　　　　xiǎo jiě　　**Noun: Miss**

小姐，请问电梯在哪儿？
xiǎo jiě qǐng wèn diàn tī zài nǎ ér

Miss, may I ask where is the elevator?

404 小朋友　　　　xiǎo péng yǒu　**Noun: children**

公园里有一群小朋友在玩。
gōng yuán lǐ yǒu yī qún xiǎo péng yǒu zài wán

A group of **children** (little friend) are playing in the park.

405 小时　　　　　xiǎo shí　　**Noun: hour**

我每天工作八个小时。
wǒ měi tiān gōng zuò bā gè xiǎo shí

I work eight **hours** a day.

406 小学　　　　　xiǎo xué　　**Noun: primary school**

我的女儿今年上小学一年级。
wǒ de nǚ ér jīn nián shàng xiǎo xué yī nián jí

My daughter attends year one in **primary school** this year.

407 小学生　　　　xiǎo xué shēng　**Noun: primary school student**

操场上有几个小学生在踢球。
cāo chǎng shàng yǒu jǐ gè xiǎo xué shēng zài tī qiú

A few **primary school students** are playing football on the playground.

408 笑   xiào   **Verb: laugh; smile**

他 的 笑 话 让 大 家 笑 了 很 久 。
tā de xiào huà ràng dà jiā xiào le hěn jiǔ

His **jokes** made everyone **laugh** for a long time.

409 写   xiě   **Verb: to write**

他 很 浪 漫 , 常 常 写 诗 。
tā hěn làng màn cháng cháng xiě shī

He is very romantic and often **writes** poems.

410 谢谢   xiè xie   **Phrase: thank you**

谢 谢 你 们 的 支 持 !
xiè xie nǐ men de zhī chí

Thank you for your support!

411 新   xīn   **Adjective: new**

我 们 打 算 买 一 辆 新 车 。
wǒ men dǎ suàn mǎi yī liàng xīn chē

We plan to buy a **new** car.

412 新年   xīn nián   **Noun: new year**

祝 大 家 新 年 快 乐 , 身 体 健 康 !
zhù dà jiā xīn nián kuài lè shēn tǐ jiàn kāng

I wish everyone a happy **new year** and have good health!

413 星期   xīng qī   **Noun: day of the week**

我 忘 了 今 天 是 星 期 几 。
wǒ wàng le jīn tiān shì xīng qī jǐ

I forgot what **day of the week** it is today.

414 星期日   xīng qī rì   **Noun: Sunday**

今 天 是 星 期 日 ，他 们 要 去 教 堂 。
jīn tiān shì xīng qī rì   tā men yào qù jiào táng

Today is **Sunday** and they are going to church.

415 星期天   xīng qī tiān   **Noun: Sunday**

我 每 星 期 天 早 上 有 中 文 课 。
wǒ měi xīng qī tiān zǎo shàng yǒu zhōng wén kè

I have Chinese class every **Sunday** morning.

416 行   xíng   **Adjective: OK**

我 想 借 你 的 车 ，行 吗 ？
wǒ xiǎng jiè nǐ de chē xíng ma

I want to borrow your car, **OK**?

417 休息   xiū xi   **Verb: to rest**

我 觉 得 很 累 ，想 早 点 休 息 。
wǒ jué dé hěn lèi xiǎng zǎo diǎn xiū xi

I feel very tired and want to **rest** early.

418 学   xué   **Verb: to learn**

我 明 年 想 学 开 车 ，你 呢 ？
wǒ míng nián xiǎng xué kāi chē nǐ ne

I want to **learn** to drive next year, how about you?

419 学生   xué sheng   **Noun: students**

这 个 大 学 有 几 千 个 学 生 。
zhè gè dà xué yǒu jǐ qiān gè xué sheng

There are thousands of **students** in this university.

420 学习　　xué xí　　**Verb: to study**

wǒ xǐ huān xué xí zhōng guó de yǔ yán hé wén huà
我 喜 欢 学 习 中 国 的 语 言 和 文 化 。
I like **studying** Chinese language and culture.

421 学校　　xué xiào　　**Noun: school**

wǒ jiě jie zài xué xiào dāng lǎo shī
我 姐 姐 在 学 校 当 老 师 。
My older sister works as a teacher in **school**.

422 学院　　xué yuàn　　**Noun: academy; college department**

tā shì wài guó yǔ xué yuàn de jiào shòu
她 是 外 国 语 学 院 的 教 授 。
She is a professor at the **academy** of Foreign Languages.

423 要　　yào　　**Verb: to want**

wǒ yào xiān qù shàng hǎi rán hòu qù guǎng zhōu
我 要 先 去 上 海 ， 然 后 去 广 州 。
I **want** to go to Shanghai first, then to Guangzhou.

424 爷爷　　yé ye　　**Noun: paternal grandpa**

xià gè yuè wǒ men huì qìng zhù yé ye de shēng rì
下 个 月 ， 我 们 会 庆 祝 爷 爷 的 生 日 。
Next month, we will celebrate **grandpa**'s birthday.

425 也　　yě　　**Adverb: also**

wǒ de nán péng yǒu yě hěn xǐ huān gǒu
我 的 男 朋 友 也 很 喜 欢 狗 。
My boyfriend **also** likes dogs very much.

426 页   yè   **Noun: page**

zhè běn shū yī gòng yǒu sān bǎi yè
这 本 书 一 共 有 三 百 页 。
This book in total has 300 **pages**.

427 一   yī   **Number: one**

nǐ néng cóng yī shǔ dào yī bǎi ma
你 能 从 一 数 到 一 百 吗 ？
Can you count from **one** to **one** hundred?

428 衣服   yī fu   **Noun: clothes**

wǒ de yī guì yǒu hěn duō piào liàng de yī fu
我 的 衣 柜 有 很 多 漂 亮 的 衣 服 。
My closet has many beautiful **clothes**.

429 医生   yī shēng   **Noun: doctor**

wǒ yào dài wǒ nǎi nai qù kàn yī shēng
我 要 带 我 奶 奶 去 看 医 生 。
I will take my grandma to see the **doctor**.

430 医院   yī yuàn   **Noun: hospital**

zhè shì wǒ men chéng shì zuì dà de yī yuàn
这 是 我 们 城 市 最 大 的 医 院 。
This is the largest **hospital** in our city.

431 一半   yī bàn   **Noun: half**

wǒ gāng gāng chī le yī bàn yuè bǐng
我 刚 刚 吃 了 一 半 月 饼 。
I just ate **half** of a mooncake.

432 一会儿 yī huǐ'r **Noun: a while**

<ruby>我<rt>wǒ</rt></ruby> <ruby>想<rt>xiǎng</rt></ruby> <ruby>坐<rt>zuò</rt></ruby> <ruby>在<rt>zài</rt></ruby> <ruby>沙<rt>shā</rt></ruby> <ruby>发<rt>fā</rt></ruby> <ruby>上<rt>shàng</rt></ruby> <ruby>休<rt>xiū</rt></ruby> <ruby>息<rt>xi</rt></ruby> <ruby>一<rt>yī</rt></ruby> <ruby>会<rt>huǐ</rt></ruby> <ruby>儿<rt>er</rt></ruby> 。

I want to sit in the sofa to rest for **a while**.

433 一块 yī kuài **Noun: a piece; a slice**

<ruby>她<rt>tā</rt></ruby> <ruby>为<rt>wèi</rt></ruby> <ruby>我<rt>wǒ</rt></ruby> <ruby>切<rt>qiē</rt></ruby> <ruby>了<rt>le</rt></ruby> <ruby>一<rt>yī</rt></ruby> <ruby>块<rt>kuài</rt></ruby> <ruby>蛋<rt>dàn</rt></ruby> <ruby>糕<rt>gāo</rt></ruby> 。

She cut **a slice** of cake for me.

434 一下 yī xià **Noun: a bit**

<ruby>对<rt>duì</rt></ruby> <ruby>不<rt>bù</rt></ruby> <ruby>起<rt>qǐ</rt></ruby> ，<ruby>我<rt>wǒ</rt></ruby> <ruby>要<rt>yào</rt></ruby> <ruby>考<rt>kǎo</rt></ruby> <ruby>虑<rt>lǜ</rt></ruby> <ruby>一<rt>yī</rt></ruby> <ruby>下<rt>xià</rt></ruby> 。

Sorry, I have to consider it **a bit**.

435 一样 yī yàng **Adjective: same**

<ruby>他<rt>tā</rt></ruby> <ruby>跟<rt>gēn</rt></ruby> <ruby>我<rt>wǒ</rt></ruby> <ruby>一<rt>yī</rt></ruby> <ruby>样<rt>yàng</rt></ruby> <ruby>喜<rt>xǐ</rt></ruby> <ruby>欢<rt>huān</rt></ruby> <ruby>中<rt>zhōng</rt></ruby> <ruby>国<rt>guó</rt></ruby> <ruby>文<rt>wén</rt></ruby> <ruby>化<rt>huà</rt></ruby> 。

He likes Chinese culture the **same** as I do.

436 一边 yī biān **Noun: one side** **Adverb: indicate simultaneous action**

Noun
<ruby>有<rt>yǒu</rt></ruby> <ruby>个<rt>gè</rt></ruby> <ruby>翻<rt>fān</rt></ruby> <ruby>译<rt>yì</rt></ruby> <ruby>站<rt>zhàn</rt></ruby> <ruby>在<rt>zài</rt></ruby> <ruby>他<rt>tā</rt></ruby> <ruby>的<rt>de</rt></ruby> <ruby>一<rt>yī</rt></ruby> <ruby>边<rt>biān</rt></ruby> 。

There is a translator standing at his **side**.

Adverb
<ruby>他<rt>tā</rt></ruby> <ruby>一<rt>yī</rt></ruby> <ruby>边<rt>biān</rt></ruby> <ruby>看<rt>kàn</rt></ruby> <ruby>电<rt>diàn</rt></ruby> <ruby>视<rt>shì</rt></ruby> ，<ruby>一<rt>yī</rt></ruby> <ruby>边<rt>biān</rt></ruby> <ruby>吃<rt>chī</rt></ruby> <ruby>饭<rt>fàn</rt></ruby> 。

He is eating **while** watching TV.

437 一点(儿)　　　yī diǎn er　　　**Noun: a little**

wǒ de dù zi yǒu yī diǎn er bù shū fú
我 的 肚 子 有 一 点 儿 不 舒 服 。
My stomach feels **a little** uncomfortable.

438 一起　　　yī qǐ　　　**Adverb: together**

wǒ míng tiān wǎn shàng huì gēn tā yī qǐ kàn diàn yǐng
我 明 天 晚 上 会 跟 他 一 起 看 电 影 。
Tomorrow night I will watch a movie **together** with him.

439 一些　　　yī xiē　　　**Noun: some**

bàn gōng shì de zhuō zi shàng yǒu yī xiē wén jiàn
办 公 室 的 桌 子 上 有 一 些 文 件 。
There are **some** documents on the desk in the office.

440 用　　　yòng　　　**Verb: to use**

wǒ kě yǐ yòng nǐ de diàn nǎo ma
我 可 以 用 你 的 电 脑 吗 ?
May I **use** your computer?

441 有　　　yǒu　　　**Verb: to have**

tā shì gōng sī de dà lǎo bǎn yǒu hěn duō qián
他 是 公 司 的 大 老 板 , 有 很 多 钱 。
He is the big boss of the company, **has** a lot of money.

442 有的　　　　　yǒu de　　　　**Pronoun: some**

yǒu de tóng shì xǐ huān tā　yǒu de tóng shì bù xǐ
有 的 同 事 喜 欢 他 ，有 的 同 事 不 喜
huān tā
欢 他 。

Some colleagues like him, and **some** dislike him.

443 有名　　　　　yǒu míng　　　　**Adjective: famous**

zhè gè fǎ guó qiú xīng hěn yǒu míng
这 个 法 国 球 星 很 有 名 。

This French football star is very **famous**.

444 有时候　　　　yǒu shí hòu　　　　**Phrase: sometimes**

zài zhōu mò wǒ yǒu shí hòu qù qí zì xíng chē
在 周 末 ，我 有 时 候 去 骑 自 行 车 。

On weekends, I **sometimes** go cycling.

445 有(一)些　　　yǒu yī xiē　　　　**Noun: a few; some**

yǒu yī xiē tóng xué qù cān jiā wǎng qiú bǐ sài le
有 一 些 同 学 去 参 加 网 球 比 赛 了 。

A few classmates went to watch the tennis match.

446 有用　　　　　yǒu yòng　　　　**Adjective: useful**

wǒ jué dé xǐ wǎn jī zuì yǒu yòng
我 觉 得 洗 碗 机 最 有 用 ！

I think the dishwasher is the most **useful**!

447 右   yòu   **Noun: right**

wǒ gèng xí guàn yòng yòu shǒu
我 更 习 惯 用 右 手 。
I am more used to using my **right** hand.

448 右边   yòu biān   **Noun: right side**

shā fā de yòu biān yǒu yī tiáo gǒu
沙 发 的 右 边 有 一 条 狗 。
There is a dog on the **right side** of the sofa.

449 雨   yǔ   **Noun: rain**

jīn tiān de yǔ tài dà le wǒ bù xiǎng chū qù
今 天 的 雨 太 大 了 , 我 不 想 出 去 。
The **rain** is too heavy today, I don't want to go out.

450 元   yuán   **Noun: monetary unit**

wǒ huā le bā qiān yuán mǎi le zhè gè xīn shǒu jī
我 花 了 八 千 元 买 了 这 个 新 手 机 。
I spent 8 thousand **yuan (CNY)** to buy this new phone.

451 远   yuǎn   **Adjective: far**

wǒ de jiā lí fēi jī chǎng hěn yuǎn
我 的 家 离 飞 机 场 很 远 。
My house is very **far** from the airport.

452 月　　　yuè　　　**Noun: month; moon**

yī nián yǒu shí èr gè yuè
一 年 有 十 二 个 月 。
There are twelve **months** in a year.

zhōng qiū jié de yuè liàng hěn měi
中 秋 节 的 月 亮 很 美 。
The moon on the Mid-Autumn Festival is beautiful.

453 再　　　zài　　　**Adverb: again**

míng nián xià tiān wǒ men xiǎng zài qù fǎ guó
明 年 夏 天 我 们 想 再 去 法 国 。
We want to go to France **again** next summer.

454 再见　　　zài jiàn　　　**Phrase: goodbye**

ér zi qù gēn nǐ shū shu shuō zài jiàn
儿 子 , 去 跟 你 叔 叔 说 再 见 。
Son, go and say **goodbye** to your uncle.

455 在　　　zài　　　**Preposition: in; at**
Verb: action in progress

Pre.
qǐng wèn zhè gè bìng rén zài nǎ gè fáng jiān
请 问 , 这 个 病 人 在 哪 个 房 间 ?
Excuse me, which room is this patient **in**?

Verb
tā zài shàng kè nǐ bù yào dǎ rǎo
她 在 上 课 , 你 不 要 打 扰 。
She **is** having lessons, don't disturb.

456 在家　　　zài jiā　　　**Verb: at home**

tā zài jiā shàng bān
他 在 家 上 班 。
He works **at home**.

457 早   zǎo   **Adjective: early**

<small>měi gè xīng qī wǔ   wǒ men dōu xià bān dé zǎo</small>
每 个 星 期 五 , 我 们 都 下 班 得 早 。

Every Friday, we finish work **early**.

458 早饭   zǎo fàn   **Noun: breakfast**

<small>wǒ de zǎo fàn shì jiān jǐ dàn hé xiāng cháng</small>
我 的 早 饭 是 煎 鸡 蛋 和 香 肠 。

My **breakfast** is fried eggs and sausages.

459 早上   zǎo shàng   **Noun: morning**

<small>wǒ měi tiān zǎo shàng bā diǎn chī zǎo fàn</small>
我 每 天 早 上 八 点 吃 早 饭 。

I have breakfast at eight every **morning**.

460 怎么   zěn me   **Pronoun: how**

<small>qǐng wèn zěn me qù dì tiě zhàn</small>
请 问 , 怎 么 去 地 铁 站 ?

Excuse me, **how** to go to the subway station?

461 站   zhàn   **Noun: station**

<small>shì zhōng xīn yǒu liǎng gè huǒ chē zhàn</small>
市 中 心 有 两 个 火 车 站 。

There are two train **stations** in the city center.

462 找   zhǎo   **Verb: to find**

<small>tā diū le shǒu jī   wǒ men zài bāng tā zhǎo</small>
她 丢 了 手 机 , 我 们 在 帮 她 找 。

She lost her mobile phone and we are helping her **find** it.

463 找到   zhǎo dào   **Verb: to have found**

tā zài shā fā shàng zhǎo dào le tā de shǒu jī
她 在 沙 发 上 找 到 了 她 的 手 机 。
She **found** her mobile phone on the sofa.

464 这   zhè   **Pronoun: this**

dà jiā hǎo zhè shì wǒ de zhōng guó péng yǒu xiǎo míng
大 家 好 , 这 是 我 的 中 国 朋 友 小 明 。
Hello everyone, **this** is my Chinese friend Xiao Ming.

465 这边   zhè biān   **Pronoun: this (side)**

zhè biān shì rén shì bù mén wǒ men jìn qù ba
这 边 是 人 事 部 门 , 我 们 进 去 吧 。
This (side) is the HR department, let's go in.

466 这里   zhè lǐ   **Pronoun: here**

wǒ hěn xǐ huān zhè lǐ de fàn cài
我 很 喜 欢 这 里 的 饭 菜 。
I like the dishes **here very much**.

467 这儿   zhè'er   **Pronoun: this place; here**

nǐ kàn zhè er jiù shì shì zhōng xīn de gōng yuán
你 看 , 这 儿 就 是 市 中 心 的 公 园 。
You see, **this** is the park of the city center.

468 这些   zhè xiē   **Pronoun: these**

zhè xiē shì mǎi gěi jiā rén de shèng dàn lǐ wù
这 些 是 买 给 家 人 的 圣 诞 礼 物 。
These are Christmas gifts for my family.

469 着 zhe **indicate continued action**

外 面 现 在 正 下 着 雨 。
wài miàn xiàn zài zhèng xià zhe yǔ

It's raining outside right now.

470 真 zhēn **Adverb: truly**

这 个 男 生 真 帅 ！
zhè gè nán shēng zhēn shuài

This guy is **truly** handsome!

471 真的 zhēn de **Adjective: true**

这 个 新 闻 是 真 的 吗 ？
zhè gè xīn wén shì zhēn de ma

Is this news **true**?

472 正 zhèng **Adverb: exactly**

这 件 衬 衫 正 是 我 想 买 的 。
zhè jiàn chèn shān zhèng shì wǒ xiǎng mǎi de

This shirt is **exactly** what I want to buy.

473 正在 zhèng zài **indicate action in progress**

我 看 见 他 的 时 候 ，他 正 在 开 车 。
wǒ kàn jiàn tā de shí hòu tā zhèng zài kāi chē

When I saw him, he **was** driving.

474 知道 zhī dào **Verb: to know**

我 知 道 公 司 不 准 室 内 抽 烟 。
wǒ zhī dào gōng sī bù zhǔn shì nèi chōu yān

I **know** that the company does not allow smoking indoors.

475 知识　zhī shí　**Noun: knowledge**

他 知 道 很 多 科 学 知 识 。
tā zhī dào hěn duō kē xué zhī shí

He knows a lot of scientific **knowledge**.

476 中　zhōng　**Preposition: amidst**
Noun: middle

Pre.
施 工 进 行 中 ， 请 绕 道 。
shī gōng jìn xíng zhōng qǐng rào dào

Construc tion work **in progress**, please detour.

Noun
他 穿 中 号 的 衣 服 。
tā chuān zhōng hào de yī fú

He wears **medium** (middle number) sized clothes.

477 中国　zhōng guó　**Noun: China**

我 打 算 明 年 去 中 国 旅 游 。
wǒ dǎ suàn míng nián qù zhōng guó lǚ yóu

I plan to travel to **China** next year.

478 中间　zhōng jiān　**Noun: middle**

在 飞 机 上 , 我 不 喜 欢 坐 中 间 的 座 位 。
zài fēi jī shàng wǒ bù xǐ huān zuò zhōng jiān de zuò wèi

On the airplane, I don't like sitting in the **middle** seat.

479 中文　zhōng wén　**Noun: Chinese language**

中 文 是 一 种 很 美 的 语 言 。
zhōng wén shì yī zhǒng hěn měi de yǔ yán

Chinese is a type of beautiful language.

480 中午 zhōng wǔ **Noun: noon**

今天中午，我会和同事吃午饭。
jīn tiān zhōng wǔ, wǒ huì hé tóng shì chī wǔ fàn

At **noon** today, I will have lunch with my colleagues.

481 中学 zhōng xué **Noun: middle school**

这个中学有一百年的历史。
zhè gè zhōng xué yǒu yī bǎi nián de lì shǐ

This **middle school** has a hundred years' history.

482 中学生 zhōng xué shēng **Noun: middle school students**

体育馆有五十个中学生。
tǐ yù guǎn yǒu wǔ shí gè zhōng xué shēng

There are fifty **middle school students** in the gymnasium.

483 重 zhòng **Adjective: heavy**

这些书很重，你需要帮忙吗？
zhè xiē shū hěn zhòng, nǐ xū yào bāng máng ma

These books are **heavy**, do you need help?

484 重要 zhòng yào **Adjective: important**

我的先生是我最重要的人。
wǒ de xiān sheng shì wǒ zuì zhòng yào de rén

My husband is the most **important** person to me.

485 住 zhù **Verb: live (at)**

你住在哪儿？我可以送你回家。
nǐ zhù zài nǎ ér? wǒ kě yǐ sòng nǐ huí jiā

Where do you **live**? I can accompany you home.

486 准备　　zhǔn bèi　　**Verb: to prepare**

míng tiān miàn shì, nǐ zhǔn bèi le ma?
明 天 面 试 , 你 准 备 了 吗 ？

For tomorrow's interview, have you **prepared**?

487 桌子　　zhuō zi　　**Noun: table**

wǒ de chú fáng yǒu yī zhāng dà yuán zhuō zi 。
我 的 厨 房 有 一 张 大 圆 桌 子 。

There is a big round **table** in my kitchen.

488 字　　zì　　**Noun: characters**

tā huì yòng máo bǐ xiě hàn zì 。
他 会 用 毛 笔 写 汉 字 。

He can write Chinese **characters** with a brush.

489 子　　zi　　**Suffix: added after nouns**

zài zhōng guó, nán shēng dài lǜ mào zi shì jìn jì 。
在 中 国 , 男 生 戴 绿 帽 子 是 禁 忌 。

In China, it is taboo for guys to wear green **hat**.

490 走　　zǒu　　**Verb: go; leave**

yǐ jīng shí diǎn le, wǒ yīng gāi zǒu le 。
已 经 十 点 了 , 我 应 该 走 了 。

It's ten o'clock, I should **go**.

491 走路　　zǒu lù　　**Verb: to walk**

gōng sī hěn jìn, suǒ yǐ wǒ měi tiān zǒu lù shàng bān 。
公 司 很 近 , 所 以 我 每 天 走 路 上 班 。

The company is very close, so I **walk** to work every day.

100

492 最   zuì   **Adverb: most**

我 觉 得 中 餐 最 好 吃！
wǒ jué dé zhōng cān zuì hǎo chī

I think Chinese food is the **most** delicious!

493 最好   zuì hǎo   **Adjective: best**

我 的 狗 是 我 最 好 的 朋 友！
wǒ de gǒu shì wǒ zuì hǎo de péng yǒu

My dog is my **best** friend!

494 最后   zuì hòu   **Noun: end; final**

你 知 道 故 事 的 最 后 是 什 么 吗？
nǐ zhī dào gù shì de zuì hòu shì shén me ma

Do you know what the **end** of the story was?

495 昨天   zuó tiān   **Noun: yesterday**

我 忘 了 昨 天 是 她 的 生 日 。
wǒ wàng le zuó tiān shì tā de shēng rì

I forgot that **yesterday** was her birthday.

496 左   zuǒ   **Noun: left**

我 习 惯 用 左 手 。
wǒ xí guàn yòng zuǒ shǒu

I am used to using my **left** hand.

497 左边   zuǒ biān   **Noun: left side**

左 边 的 房 间 是 我 的 卧 室 。
zuǒ biān de fáng jiān shì wǒ de wò shì

The room on the **left side** is my bedroom.

498 坐   zuò   Verb: to take (vehicle); to sit

wǒ dǎ suàn zuò fēi jī qù běi jīng
我 打 算 坐 飞 机 去 北 京 。
I plan to **take** plane to Beijing.

xiān shēng nín hǎo qǐng zuò
先 生 您 好 ！ 请 坐 。
Hello sir! Please **sit**.

499 坐下   zuò xià   Verb: to sit down

qǐng nǐ xiān zuò xià wǒ mǎ shàng jiù huí lái
请 你 先 坐 下 ， 我 马 上 就 回 来 。
Please **sit down** first, I will be back soon.

500 做   zuò   Verb: to make; to do; to be

wǒ hěn xǐ huān zuò jiǎo zi
我 很 喜 欢 做 饺 子 。
I like **making** dumplings very much.

wǒ ér zi shuō zhǎng dà hòu yào zuò fēi xíng yuán
我 儿 子 说 ， 长 大 后 要 做 飞 行 员 。
My son said that, he wants **to be** a pilot when he grows up.

ACCESS AUDIO

I highly encourage you to use the accompanying audio recordings for all of the examples in this book, not only will it help to improve your listening skills but if you are unfamiliar or unsure about the pronunciations of any words in this book, then you can listen to them spoken by native speakers.

INSTRUCTIONS TO ACCESS AUDIO

1. **Scan this QR code** ──────────►
   or go to: **www.linglingmandarin.com/books**

2. Locate this book in the list of LingLing Mandarin Books

3. Click the "Access Audio" button

   Access Audio

4. Enter the password (case-sensitive):

Yc7s6Kh

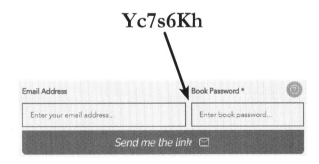

GET YOUR FREE EBOOK NOW

linglingmandarin.com/beginner-bundle

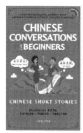
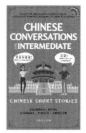

CHINESE
CONVERSATIONS
FOR BEGINNERS

CHINESE
CONVERSATIONS
FOR INTERMEDIATE

LEARN CHINESE
VOCABULARY
FOR BEGINNERS
(NEW HSK 1)

CHINESE STORIES
FOR LANGUAGE
LEARNERS:
ELEMENTARY

CHINESE STORIES
FOR LANGUAGE
LEARNERS:
INTERMEDIATE

THE ART OF WAR
FOR LANGUAGE
LEARNERS

MANADARIN
WRITING
PRACTICE BOOK

LEARN CHINESE
VOCABULARY FOR
BEGINNERS
(NEW HSK 2)

LEARN CHINESE
VOCABULARY FOR
BEGINNERS
(NEW HSK 3)

Get notified about **new releases**
https://linglingmandarin.com/notify

ABOUT THE AUTHOR

LingLing is a native Chinese Mandarin educator with an MA in Communication and Language. Originally from China, now living in the UK, she is the founder of the learning brand LingLing Mandarin, which aims to create the best resources for learners to master the Chinese language and achieve deep insight into Chinese culture in a fun and illuminating way. *Discover more about LingLing and access more great resources by following the links below or scanning the QR codes.*

 WEBSITE
linglingmandarin.com

YOUTUBE CHANNEL
youtube.com/c/linglingmandarin

 PATREON
patreon.com/linglingmandarin

INSTAGRAM
instagram.com/linglingmandarin

Made in the USA
Las Vegas, NV
08 September 2023